The Art of
Social Climbing
A Guide for the Socially Ambitious

LINCOLN KERNEY

ISBN: 1495441865
ISBN 13: 9781495441868
Library of Congress Control Number: 2014902712
CreateSpace Independent Publishing Platform
North Charleston, South Carolina

Note

The purpose of this book is not to hurt or insult anyone. Consequently, some of the names, places, and circumstances have been slightly altered. The purpose is to help those with social aspirations better achieve their goals.

Social climbers get a bad rap. I dabbled myself in the art of it, so I know. They are fascinating to watch. Many fall by the wayside, but others go the whole way and end up as old guard to everyone except the real old guard.

—Gus Bailey in *Too Much Money* by Dominick Dunne

Table of Contents

Introduction ix

First and Foremost 1

Household Help 8

Your Background 14

At Home 20

On Vacation 26

Traveling 31

Charities, Volunteering, and Common Interests 36

Marrying Up 42

You Can't Get Away with It 48

Name-Dropping, Bragging, Bigotry, and Gossip 53

How to (and How Not to) Dress 58

Dinner Conversation and Entertaining 63

You Are What You Eat 68

The Rich Do Economize 71

The Little Darlings (Children and Pets) 75

The Power behind the Throne 80

In Funds We Trust 84

Important Things to Know 88

Appendices   93
  Accoutrements for Social Climbers   95
  Things Social Climbers Should Avoid   97
  Old-Money Staples   99

Introduction

There are many people who think that those lucky folks who have had money all their lives—or money that their family has had for generations—are usually dysfunctional. Really, these people just function in their own world, with their own rules. Every stratus of society, from the very rich to the homeless, has to have rules to keep their world alive and functioning. This only makes them appear dysfunctional to outsiders. Within their own realms, they function very well.

People may think that old-moneyed people are shallow and snobs. Sometimes this is true. But to function properly in the world of old money, which is different from the everyday world, there have to be different rules and standards. It is not just a matter of preserving this world. It is a matter of preserving the hierarchy that has governed humankind from prehistoric times. There has always been a class system, and there always will be. Old money is not dysfunctional; it just functions differently.

The author was lucky enough to be born into a socially prominent family. His great-grandparents arrived in this country in the midnineteenth century. His grandfather lived the American dream and, with the help of his wife's small inheritance and a lot of acumen, founded a business in the Northeast that would carry the family for generations. With his money, civic undertaking, and great charm, he was a natural social climber. The family spent the winters in Palm Beach and the summers at the shore, and lived well.

The author's uncle Tim, unfortunately, married his second wife, Olivia (née Olive), a woman of questionable moral character. She attempted to be a social climber, but her base character was so ingrained that she failed. She went places, due to her husband's station, but she was never accepted. Fortunately for her, she spent her last twenty years in Palm Beach, where social climbing was almost a sport and where there were many playing levels.

We are living in a time when more vast fortunes are being made faster than at any time in the last one hundred years. Although wealth will open many doors, there are those that will remain closed to new money. These doors, both home and club, are closed to all but those whom the old moneyed feel comfortable with. For some reason, that makes those within these doors very desirable company for a certain type of new money.

There are people who make fortunes, and they are quite happy to spend it their way. The more vulgar the display of their money, the happier they are. They love to build the biggest house with gold bathroom fixtures and have fountains cascading in their front courtyard. They strive for publicity, and when they are photographed, they are wearing clothes that would be at home at the Oscars, glittering with jewels. They don't care if they are crass and common; after all, they are rich, rich, rich.

There are others who make their fortunes and are quite happy not showing anything off. They may or may not move to a better house. When they buy a new car, they may stick with the same make. They are quite comfortable with themselves. Often, they earn the respect of old money for not caring; after all, that is the whole game. They are then "in" with old money, if they so choose.

And then there are social climbers. Through the ages they have been celebrated on the stage, on film, and in literature. They certainly have nothing to be ashamed of. After all, they are the American dream. It is better to be new money than no money. They were not born with money, but they admire people with old money and want to associate with them. First they have to learn the rules of the game. In the game of high society, all information, both useful and useless, is vitally important. You have to know what to do, how to do it correctly, and where to do it. And you have to know who is doing what and who has done what. It is never too late to learn. If you have reached the zenith of what you imagine is your social dreamland, you still can make gaffes if you are not practiced. Many who arrive unprepared do not retain their status because they have not properly conditioned themselves. Any misstep or mistake can unceremoniously dethrone you. The cruel thing is this: in polite society, no one will ever tell you about your errors. They will note them and discuss them but will let you figure out your own shortcomings. And you may never learn why people don't include you in intimate dinner parties or on group trips. You will slowly be eased to the side, no matter how many parties you have or how well you dress.

To be sure, unless both partners are ready to social climb, it can ruin a marriage. If, for instance, the wife is all about social climbing but the husband works hard all week and wants to spend the weekends jogging and watching television, it can wear their marriage down. Ditto if the man wants to get ahead socially, maybe for business reasons. If his wife is no good at the game, he is lost. Resentment follows, as does probably either an affair or divorce. Usually, even with women making strides in the workplace, women make the social decisions, and the men follow along. It is really up to the woman to make the social connections, even if she is working full time. Other than sports at their club, men don't have many chances to make connections, and even if Joe meets Ben at the club while playing golf, unless their wives know each other, they probably won't see each other elsewhere.

All people are born equal. Money cannot buy good taste and good manners. Old money isn't born with good taste or good manners either. They are learned every moment of every day, from birth until they become a way of life. People with old money are just educated at a different level. They grow up with etiquette lessons twenty-four hours a day. They are often coached in sports, in dancing, in grace, in fine living, and in how to dress so as not to appear that they care too much. It is part of their core. They know where to go and when to go there. They learn what to eat and drink, how to tip, and how to converse. A very important part of social climbing is to remain true to yourself and to be confident and comfortable with who you are. Part of old money's education is how to be part of the upper class (and yes, there is one) without trying.

With the help of this book, you can, too.

1

First and Foremost

*I*t goes without saying that the foundation of social climbing is money. It is really no good without it. The old rich, of course, want to protect their money. But they also know that it is there to have fun with, not to display or impress. If that happens, so be it, but it is not the goal. In the old days, people didn't really care about money. Either you were wellborn or not. Of course, there were those who made so much money—or who combined a lot of money with civic duty—that they could not be ignored. If you really have your heart set on climbing, make or marry a lot of money. While you do, though, there are many other steps you can take.

First and foremost, good manners are a key. As my grandfather, the founder of the family fortune, said, "Always keep it simple, never get high-hat, a pleasant word costs nothing, and good manners cannot be put on for state occasions. If you are not polite to the waitress, you will sometimes fail to be polite to the hostess. And, as Kipling remarked, they are all alike under the skin. Industry and good manners are the best of all virtues."

I cringe when I am at a restaurant or a club and someone is dressing down the waiter or waitress or berating the manager in public. It is never necessary and is always unattractive to be condescending. Even if you feel superior, keep it to yourself. It can be your little secret. If someone is condescending to you, you can bet that he or she is not the real McCoy. People brought up well are unfailingly polite, even if they feel otherwise. It is not hypocritical to be polite to someone you do not care for or, worse, who is rude. It is good manners.

There are many books that you can study and courses that you can take to learn the subtlety of good manners. I remember one of the first things my aunt Olivia did was to read Emily Post. It did not take, however. Until her death, over forty years later, she remained as coarse and common as the day she arrived in Bar Harbor with Uncle Tim. They had wed on their way up, without telling anyone. Tim's children were staying with family friends. It was a shock to the friends; it was devastating to the children. And when they returned home, my grandmother relieved Uncle Tim of his corporate duties and the salary that went therewith.

When you study good manners, remember this: a dead giveaway is someone who is too pointed about their manners. Old money is brought up with good manners. It is part of their core. The main thing to remember about manners is that they are based on consideration. If you are considerate of another person, it is half the battle. Emily Post and others merely refined this into rules. They are, however, rules that should be ingrained into you so that you do not hesitate. To hesitate is to show weakness. Never be weak or unsure. Also, never point out someone else's lack of good manners. Remember: be considerate. If someone uses the wrong utensil or glass or does not put the finger bowl to the side, say nothing and, if necessary, turn away.

A friend of mine was presiding over a dinner in her stepfather's dining room. Her mother had died a year earlier, and the stepfather decided it was time to get back in circulation. Her mother's finest crystal, china, and linens were used for the white-tie dinner. At one point, she turned to the elderly gentleman next to her, only to have him proceed to blow his nose into one of the damask napkins. She merely turned to the gentleman on the other side and started a conversation as he dripped soup down his front. There was nothing to do but remain steadfastly polite as a footman came to his aid.

Never be demanding. It is embarrassing for others if you are rude to a waiter or snap you fingers at a waitress. If necessary, a gentleman will rise from the table and go ask the server to please come to the table when possible. This is done in a quiet and unobtrusive manner.

Also, when dining out, unless the food is truly terrible, it is not good to send it back. Especially if you are a guest, it is an insult to the host. To repeatedly send food back is an affront to the chef but also to your fellow diners. It really doesn't show that you are used to the right things. It shows how you are unused to being in polite society.

It is all right to let management know if something is not up to your expectations. Unless someone tells them, they don't know. A friend of mine was head of the house committee at our eating club. It seemed that whenever he was there, there was something that could have been better: the service or the food or the overall cleanliness of the club. I mentioned once to the club manager about his constant comments. The manager said, "We appreciate

Mr. Williams's comments so that we can get the club up to where it should be." But if you are going to comment to management, do so without making a fuss. Either call or drop them an e-mail the next day.

It is important if you are staying at someone's house to treat the help with the utmost respect and courtesy. Often, the help has been part of the family for years. And they can be both very protective of the family and real snobs in their own right. The worst thing to have happen is to have a trusted employee rat you out as an impostor. No matter how large the staff, pick up your own clothes and make your bed. Over time, it is fine to get chummy with the staff—but not familiar. They will know what to call you; do not say, "Oh, please call me *Mary*." Never pry about the other servants or the hosting family. It is fine to ask their opinion about something, but if you pry, they may lie. And they will tell. No matter what you think about your hosting family, a good staff member remains tight-lipped and very loyal to his or her employers. And tip them well: plan on at least ten dollars a night, with a bonus if they give special service, such as pressing clothes or getting forgotten toiletries.

Also, never be late for meals or other events. It shows lack of consideration. If a family member is late, he or she will be dealt with. If a guest is late, and repeatedly so, he or she may not be invited back.

It is best not to make suggestions or plans for your hosts without telling them. Once a fellow from Tennessee was visiting his fiancée's family in Connecticut for the weekend. He had never been there. While the family was otherwise occupied, he was sitting on the terrace. The housekeeper brought him some lemonade as the squirrels frolicked in the garden. He said, "You know, Minnie, where I come from, we eat those things. They are a delicacy." She said

"Oh, yes, Master Thomas. We do, too, in North Carolina." He said, "Minnie, I have the recipe. If I shot some of those, would you cook them for dinner?" "Oh, yes," she replied. It was not a pleasant dining experience when, at the end of the meal, the truth came out. Minnie and the master Thomas thought they had given the family a wonderful experience. Diners ran from the table, horrified, with napkins covering their mouths.

If you know that you are going to take in some extra events over the weekend—like a dinner dance at someone's house or a golf tournament at the club—it is fine to ask what the dress is. It is never good to overdress, especially in summer. And it is vulgar to wear inappropriate jewelry or finery. On the matter of clothing, it is always wise to be a little understated. Keep in mind where you will be. You will probably not wear the same clothes in Palm Beach as Mustique. You will not have the same wardrobe for a hunting plantation as a weekend house on Long Island.

For that matter, keep in mind *where* you are social climbing. It is well-known that Boston and Philadelphia and some Southern cities (like Charleston) are almost impossible for anyone who is not a local or who has not been properly introduced to be accepted. However, just about every city and town has its old families. While many people think of Los Angeles as Hollywood, Beverly Hills, and Bel Air, the really old money is generally in Pasadena and Hancock Park. You have to choose, however, if you are going for the glitz, which may be much easier, or for the established.

Texas is another place where people make the mistake of thinking that all you need is money. Before big oil, there was ranching and entrepreneurship. There is big money in Texas, and it is as old and refined as any in the East. It is just quieter than the new money. Due to the preponderance of new money, the two have to get along, and eventually, new money will become old. They do have rules though. And they are a very tight society when they need to circle the wagons. Billionaire T. Cullen Davis married a divorcée, Priscilla Willborn. Although they lived big for a while, Priscilla was never accepted by Fort Worth society. Eventually the marriage ended with the violent murders of Priscilla's daughter and boyfriend, Cullen being charged and spending quite a bit of his fortune to get acquitted. If you marry money, play by their rules.

Never use and drop people on the way up. It is bad form. If you befriend someone on the way up, you are really beholden to him or her. If it is someone whom you think is maybe not as far up the social ladder as you are aiming to go, he or she still has loyal friends who will notice if someone has used their friend and dropped him or her. It will not be appreciated, and the individual may be higher than you think—especially his or her connections. Once my sister and a friend thought they would try out interior design as a career. Their first (and only) client was rude and demanding. He questioned every charge and tried to go around them and deal directly with the tradespeople. He complained about every bill, even though he and his wife made all the selections. What he did not realize was that the people he was going to try to meet were the ones he was working with. At one point he said, "Have you heard of the Livingstons? We are going to meet them Saturday at a dinner party." He was right. The Livingstons were very important people at the top of the social ladder locally and in New York. They were our aunt and uncle.

Also don't think that just because you are friendly with a bunch of social climbers who were there before you that you are in society. Most whom new people think of as high society are just other social climbers. If they make you happy, so be it. But the real thing they're not. Learn to tell the difference.

2

HOUSEHOLD HELP

*T*here was a time when a household staff was as necessary for people with money as a telephone. Those days changed after the Second World War. However, if you are lucky enough to have help, there are things you should know. They are people. The days of *Gone with the Wind* or *The Help* are, thankfully, over. Never refer to them as "my maid" or "my Irish girl." Someone once said "my Irish girl" to my mother. She never forgave it, being of Irish descent herself.

As I said, the staff can be invaluable, sometimes part of the family. When Uncle Tim's circumstances were reduced, due to his unemployment, he had to cut back to a staff of one housekeeper, Margaret, who had been with the family for over twenty years. Once he walked in on Olivia, who was giving the lady a dressing down. He stopped her and said, "Olivia, if it is between you and Margaret, I am going with Margaret." There was never any more trouble. Evidently she knew he was not joking. A truce was silently declared, although familial love was never exchanged between the two. Uncle Tim and the housekeeper died within weeks of each other.

Once, it occurred to me that my grandmother and all of her six children had household staffs. There were Swedish, German, Scottish, Black, and French—but no Irish. After all, I had heard from the wasps what good maids the Irish were. I asked my mother about this. She said, "Dear, people never hire their own kind. It is too much of a reminder." It took me a while to figure out what she meant. Other than a very few, people did not arrive in America with wealth. Some hardworking immigrant or someone not too far down the line made it. To have your own kind serving you would be a reminder that there but for good fortune go you. So remember: those you are aspiring to socialize with are basically not that different from you.

Refer to help by their name; it is only polite. If you are sharing help, either a weekly cleaner or babysitters, never pay more than the going rate. Especially if you are new to town, it is unacceptable to raise the going rate that others have established, as long as it is fair. How you treat your help is also important. Treat them with respect and kindness. They are a valuable part of your life, and if they have been in the job long, they can offer invaluable assistance and sage advice, if they like you. And sometimes they can be a great source of information, if they trust you. They gather all kinds of information from servicepeople and other help. When I was growing up, we had mostly Scottish help. They were friendly with other Scots in town. There was a housekeeper up the street who worked for a couple with three children. The Second World War and rationing had been over for a decade. The couple had butter for themselves but margarine for their children and the housekeeper. And while they ate regular food, the children and housekeeper were usually fed hot dogs, which was probably why they always looked so unhealthy. Needless to say, she did not stay there long, and people did not really warm up to that couple too much.

Never think that because the help is doing what they do, they are intellectually inferior. Once I had a gardener, whom I inherited when I bought my house. His father had been the gardener before him. He knew the Latin names of all the plants. He spoke French and was a nationally renowned pipe organ player. He was one of the few people whom the local university let play their intricate pipe organ. He just liked working outside. I realized that I did not need to offer much direction. He would appear at the back door on the appointed morning and come in for coffee and a chat about what needed to be done. I might say that the hedges at the foot of the front lawn needed trimming or that the garden by the tennis court needed attention. He would then go and prune the orchard or tend to whatever he felt needed attention. I figured that he had been there for over forty years, so he knew best. He was also a wonderful bartender at dinner and Christmas parties. Anyway, for the first few years, I enjoyed working in the garden, but my allergies got the best of me. After he died, I hired a landscape service, but it was just never the same.

It is a cardinal sin to steal other people's help. Once, after a dinner party in a prominent couple's house, a guest stole into the kitchen and hired away the cook. While her menus improved vastly, no one came to her table to share them. And she was quickly dropped off of other guest lists. The result was that she packed up her household and family and moved away. The cook did not go with her.

It is also a cardinal sin to sleep with the help. Although it happens more than one would hope, it is just not a good idea. Of course, there are famous stories, such as the pharmaceutical heir who bedded his wife's upstairs maid. Eventually she became the wife—his third and last. He left her the bulk of his fortune, leading to a well-publicized and costly court battle with the children from his first two marriages. Everyone came away with fortunes but also with tarnished reputations.

But there was the Palm Beach chef who was caught in flagrante with the wife of his employer. It damaged, but did not destroy, the marriage, but the chef had to seek employment in another part of the country.

If you are fortunate enough to have a large staff, don't flaunt it. If you decide to go that route, be forewarned. Having a group of strangers living under your roof is not easy. It involves balancing staff duties with privacy issues. Old money often grew up with live-in help, so it is now second nature. You cannot invade their space, but to do their job, they have to invade yours. So, if that will upset you, set reasonable guidelines ahead of time. While staff should remain as invisible as possible, very few houses today are set up for it.

Remember to keep a sense of humor also. A friend was interviewing for a housekeeper. When she hired one, she said, "We entertain quite a bit. Are you comfortable helping with that?" The lady replied, "Oh, yes. But I have one question. Mrs. Jones, does we stack, or is we class?" The story has brought laughs to many for years. The answer to her question was "We is class." Although stacking has become a more accepted way to clear the table in familial settings, it is still frowned upon. Another faux pas is clearing the table before everyone has finished. Unfortunately, it has become a common practice in public dining establishments. It is really quite rude.

It is also rude to comment on the speed at which someone finishes his or her meal. If someone eats too quickly or too slowly, it is their digestion, not you, that should take notice.

Sometimes it is the help that has to put people in their place. Once, when I was a child, my father's sister was visiting. She was known as somewhat of a tyrant. As she went upstairs, she ran her finger across the tops of the pictures. Unfortunately, she did this just as the housekeeper entered the hall. "Would you like a duster, Mrs. Wellington?" Aunt Katherine never did that again.

I have always been a fan of blanket covers. They do not have to be fancy, lacy covers. Simple seersucker will do. I just do not like the feel of a blanket, and frankly, the thought of someone else whom I didn't even know touching and coughing on the blanket I am under is quite unsettling to me. It seems that most people do not even know what a blanket cover is. I was once in an upscale linen store where there were quite a few blanket covers. One lady suggested to her friend that she get some for her guest room. The friend asked what they were. The clerk and the lady were trying to explain. I couldn't help myself. I jumped into the conversation uninvited and said that if she ever tried a blanket cover, she wouldn't live without them. I must say, I sounded a bit deranged, but such is my regard for the blanket cover. If you don't know about them, you should acquaint yourself with them. Years ago, a test for a suspected climber was to bring out the finger bowls and see if he or she knew the somewhat archaic etiquette. I think today that even the children of the house would have little idea what to do with them. Therefore, I think today's test should be blanket covers.

Service people are others whom you need to treat well. After all, they keep your world going. We once had a curtain and slipcover maker who made no bones about who used cheap material, who shortchanged him, and who was very nice. He was the best in the business, but if he didn't like you, he didn't work for you. And if he didn't work for you, everyone knew why. Service people get around. They sometimes tell stories without naming names, but it is all too obvious whom they are talking about, especially in small communities. Plus, if you are mean and inconsiderate to the window washer, you will have dirty windows! If they don't talk to the family of the house, they will certainly talk to the servants, and then they will name names. And remember what I said about the servants ratting you out!

3

Your Background

*O*ften, social climbers feel that their background needs a little adjusting. It is usually a mistake to get too carried away with this. It is a very small world among the old rich. Never make up where you went to school or where you grew up. Rich people seem to all go to the same schools, the same resorts, the same everything, so there is a lot of crossover. People know people who know people. It is too easy to check up, even inadvertently. Unless you were a prostitute, it is unforgivable to be ashamed of your background. You are who you are. Perhaps you need a little polishing, but never reinvent yourself.

Most old money used to be Episcopalian. In New York, families would convert just so their daughter could make her debut at the right ball. Now it is not necessary for young ladies to make a debut, nor is it necessarily more acceptable to be Episcopalian. In modern times most mainstream religions are socially acceptable. However, if you are ever invited to a coming-out party, they are really quite fun. They are not as popular as they once were, but when I was in my late teens and early twenties, I quite enjoyed them. In fact, I finished up college in Texas because the parties were plentiful, and Texans know how to give a party.

A lady I was acquainted with married a social widower who had inherited quite a bit of money. At one point they moved into a large house in a fine old neighborhood. She had the house done over from top to bottom, including its nine bedrooms, which seemed excessive for the two of them. As she went from room to room, she would say, "That was my mother's" or "This was my mother's." She seemed to have forgotten where she came from, although it was no secret that she had not been raised by the manor born. Her mother ended up with five or six silver dressing-table sets. No one pointed out to her that guests usually traveled with their own brush and comb. At any rate, she had married up and had to be accepted, if not welcomed.

Language is a tricky thing here. First of all, if you do not have good grammar, get a grammar book and practice, practice, practice! While you may want to adjust your accent, never acquire one that is unsuitable. If you are from Atlantic City, don't try to speak like a Boston Brahmin. It never works, and it ends up being a linguistic roller coaster. There are words and phrases that can give you away, too. Avoid "estate" or "mansion" unless you are in real estate. Never call a building a "home." Home is where the heart is or where infirmed older people are sent, not the building where you live. In the midtwentieth century, it was not acceptable to refer to people as "wealthy." The proper adjective was "rich." That, however, seems too blunt today, although, it is certainly short and to the point. It is more acceptable to just say that people have money—or even pots of money or tons of money. The Duchess of Windsor is credited with saying, "You can never be too rich or too thin." That is probably no longer true. Eating disorders plague many American youth. Multibillionaires should probably think about setting up charitable foundations or diversifying their wealth, if only for public relations. A few billion should do to keep anyone in style.

Do not use words larger than you are comfortable using. Someone once asked a friend of mine (who lived off Sutton Place), "What is the configuration of your apartment?" It was an awkward question on several fronts. It just didn't sound natural. And the configuration was one room, as he told her. That ended that conversation. In spite of the fact that he was very social in New York, he was clearly not worth her while. It is probably not a good idea to ask too many personal questions before getting to know someone. Do not assume that just because you are seated next to someone at a dinner in Southampton or Hobe Sound that they have multiple homes. If they want to share that kind of information, they will. Except in movies, I have never heard the words "winter" and "summer" used as verbs. In speaking, be as simple and unpretentious as possible.

Nor have I ever actually heard anyone from polite society actually say "NOCD" (not our class, dear). For one thing, we don't talk about "our class." Anyone who acts the part of a snob through rudeness is insecure and probably a fake.

Don't be loud, boorish, or crude. It may get attention—the wrong kind. Speak softly. You don't have to be Jackie Kennedy, but if people have to strain a bit to hear you, it keeps their attention.

Also, when you are speaking with someone, look at him or her. As a shy child, I was always being reminded to look at people I was speaking with. It was very difficult, but it was a lesson worth learning. It is unnerving, and a bit insulting, to be talking with someone while their eyes are darting around like hummingbirds, looking to see if someone they think is more important is around. If the person you are talking with is boring, make a polite excuse to get away. Remember, however, that in your position, you may be the recipient of those excuses. Social climbers are not in a position to judge who or what is important.

If you go out to a dinner party, take the seat you are given. The host or hostess has done a specific seating arrangement for his or her own reasons. It is extremely rude to rearrange someone else's seating. And if you go to a benefit that includes a seated dinner, either put your own table together or stay in the seat you are provided. I went to a benefit in a town where I was visiting, and I was seated at dinner. I knew most of the people there, including one couple who thought they should have been at a "more important" table. She kept looking around and waving to people at other tables. Halfway through the dinner, the wife asked her husband, "Are you finished?" He replied, "I could be." She handed his plate to the server and said, "Come on," and they were out of there before dessert. It was one of the rudest displays I have ever witnessed, and it only confirmed to everyone what an aggressive social climber she was. It takes more than an Hermes bag and Belgian shoes to make a silk purse out of a sow's ear.

Proper correspondence is often overlooked. In the age of computers, writing paper often gets forgotten. It is important to have nice stationery, preferably personalized—but again, for social climbers, the simpler the better. A monogram or name and address will do. A border and lined envelopes are acceptable for ladies, not for gentlemen. While it is not necessary, it is nice to have paper from stationers like Dempsey & Carroll or Cartier or even a local purveyor. They can help with the proper selection also. However, places like Merrimade or American Stationery are acceptable, if you know what to pick.

While e-mail has become more prevalent in society, unless you are very close with someone, a written thank-you note is mandatory for gifts and certain occasions, as I'm sure whichever etiquette lessons you choose will tell you. For all house visits, both a note and a gift are proper. The gift should be equivalent to the occasion and the length of stay. Unless you are staying with family or very close friends, two nights is probably the maximum for the first stay. It can be as hard to be a guest as a host. On one visit to the home of friends in Watch Hill for the weekend, I found upon arrival that every minute of the day was planned out. The schedule was tight and the hostess unyielding. It was more exhausting than anything and did not make for a repeat experience.

A friend of mine was at the New Jersey shore, visiting people whom he thought were close friends; there was ongoing activity. Most of it was fishing, which he didn't care for. He was not pressed to join in everything, so he relaxed and read. Later, he found that they had been very insulted that he had not joined in. So you sometimes can't win, but good communication is valuable. Just remember to be polite and be yourself.

No matter how dreadful a time you have, always write an appreciative, if a bit untrue, note.

If your penmanship is illegible, please take time to get a penmanship workbook and improve it. There is a certain squared script among ladies that seems to have been learned at prep school, but you do not have to emulate this. Just a nice, clear hand will do.

Either a phone call or a note can deal with dinners. But "thank you" is a necessary phrase. If you are very close, in today's society, e-mail is getting more acceptable. However, if you are climbing, a little formality is safe.

Calling cards used to be as necessary as stationery for society folk. They are small cards with your formal name engraved. Certainly before the telephone, people used to call in person, and if the host or hostess was not home or not receiving, the card would be put on a card tray in the front hall. With the advent of the telephone, these fell out of fashion. However, they are still useful to enclose with wedding presents, flowers, and other items that are delivered to friends and acquaintances. A modern form of the calling card is a card that gives your name and contact information. Certainly, in business, cards are necessities. In everyday life it is just easier to hand someone a card rather than to tell him or her your e-mail address, phone, etc.

There was a time when a lady was only mentioned in the newspaper when she was married and when she died. Now that is not the case. However, do not seek out publicity. If it finds you, only hope that it is in the pages of the *New York Times* "Style" section and not "Page 6" of the *New York Post*. It used to be expected that a social marriage would be announced in the newspaper, especially in a large city—now, not so much. Anyone who wants to pay a small fortune can announce his or her marriage or post an obituary. Why not just take out an advertisement? Anyway, anything you want to know about a wedding will either be on the invitation or announcement list or you will read about it in an alumni magazine.

4

AT HOME

*O*ne of the first things you will want to do when you get some money is move. Whether you choose to remain in the same town or move to one that has a bit more panache, choosing a new house can be daunting. Do not make the common mistake of most new money and think that bigger and flashier is better. It is not. Think about moving into an established neighborhood. They are really much more appealing than new developments. Often these houses have interesting histories or have housed famous people. They certainly have more character than the new cookie-cutter houses. When picking a house, figure on the needs of your family and friends. There is a good chance that an older house will need remodeling. Check around for the architects with the best reputations and interview them to make sure that they are the right fit for you.

One example of an exception of this would be the late Anne Burnett Windfohr Tandy, who had I. M. Pei design his only residential commission as her house. It was quite an impressive structure that only someone with the background and presence of Mrs. Tandy could pull off. She was not only very old Texas money (Four Sixes Ranch and oil); she was one of the richest women in America and married to the founder of the Tandy Corporation. She knew exactly who she was, and even an I. M. Pei house was not considered over-the-top for her.

As I said previously, I went to college in Texas. My roommate got married after my junior year. I did not really want to find another roommate or move, and I knew that my father would not increase my allowance, so I got a part-time job at a liquor store. It was in the fashionable section of Fort Worth, and part of my duties was making some deliveries. One day I was dispatched to Mrs. Tandy's. It was my custom to go to the front door, except when I was visiting family or close friends, when I used the back or family door. So I went to Mrs. Tandy's front door. She let me in and graciously showed me where to put the order. I was blown away by the house. When I got back to the store, I relayed my impression to the owner. He was incredulous that I would go to the front door. I simply told him that although I had met Mrs. Tandy at parties, I did not feel familiar enough to go to the back door.

Many architects want to make a statement, and that statement may not fit your lifestyle. The mother of a friend wanted to build a smaller house on some land she owned. The family had a friend who was considered quite a celebrated architect. However, his style was ultracontemporary. My friend's mother had been raised in New England, had always lived in traditional houses, and had acquired beautiful art and antiques. The plans he came up with were a series of geodesic domes linked together with glass galleries. It was not what she had in mind. She paid him for the plans, moved on, and built a replica of her former summer house on Cape Cod.

A good architect can guide you to a good builder, a good landscape architect, and a good interior designer. The builder should give you an accurate estimate of cost and the time it will take for the renovation. Bob Zion, a noted landscape architect who designed Paley Park, one of the first pocket parks in Manhattan, was very reasonable for a morning's consult. He once designed a Belgian block terrace to resemble an oriental rug for a brick Georgian house. The interior designer should be on the job early on so that any ideas he or she has can be incorporated into the plans. Be careful to choose the right designer, who will not get carried away. You certainly do not want everything matching. Old money only buys some things. Most get handed down from generation to generation. Go for things with patina. Look at things as well-loved rather than as old, worn, or battered.

A new vogue seems to be to avoid "brown furniture." This seems to include almost all antiques, unfortunately. Many families have handed down beautiful furniture from generation to generation. Unfortunately, the current trend seems to be for Pottery Barn or Restoration Hardware, which is fine for young married couples starting out, but it is certainly not the classic look of an early American or English antique. This would be fashion over style. Fortunately for social climbers, it is probably a good time to buy some beautiful pieces at reasonable prices. Your decorator can either find pieces or take you to a reputable auction house. Remember: not everything has to match. You are building a collection, not a showroom. It is best to mix things up but stay within the same genre. For example, it is best not to mix country antiques with Chinese Chippendale, although it can work with the right eye. I would recommend a trip to Winterthur, Williamsburg, or some museum of like quality to see antiques in a proper setting. You do not have to be as authentic as these museums, but they will give you a good feel for lovely furniture.

Also, pay attention to your linens. Ditch the no-iron sheets. Go to a good linen shop and replace your bed linens and towels with high quality, maybe monogrammed, linens and towels. Get decent (have-to-be-ironed) table linens. Your decorator can help with this. Buy some nice sterling silver flatware for the table. Sterling is always preferred to plate in silver unless it is Sheffield. Sheffield silver was made in the eighteenth and nineteenth centuries and can command even higher prices than sterling. Usually it is in the form of candlesticks or trays and bowls. You have to remember to tell the person who polishes it not to polish it too hard. Often, silver polishers don't know Sheffield. As the plate is often worn down in places, they concentrate on polishing harder, eventually wearing all the silver off—not good.

Remember that your home is not only where you and your family live; it is also your stage for social climbing. Go easy on the overhead lights in public rooms. They are not flattering, especially as people age. And colors can either make people look good (coral, red, pink) or not good (light green). Anyway, these are points where your decorator can help out. What you are aiming for is a house that looks like it has always been that way and that will show off whatever you decide to collect.

Collecting is very important. There are endless things to collect. Whether you choose to collect art, Asian artifacts, Dresden or Staffordshire china, oriental rugs, or American antiques, make sure that you genuinely like it and learn all there is to know about it. If you choose art or artifacts, you may want to find one particular area or style to concentrate on. If you do, there are experts who can guide you. Do not collect hideous things like Kewpie dolls, tea cozies, or beer steins. They are better left to the lower classes to place in their basement recreation rooms.

While it is acceptable to have a few silk flower arrangements around, fresh flowers are a luxury you might consider. Do not purchase some ordinary florist's arrangement. Find a good florist. For a special dinner party or other occasion, you can supply your own container (silver bowl, Simon Pearce vase, or something comparable), and he or she should be able to do an arrangement that will compliment your décor. Remember, if it is going in the middle of the table, make it low enough so that people can talk over it. Don't overdo it unless you are having a wedding or a funeral. For every day, buy loose flowers and learn to arrange them yourself. For this, you can go to any flower store or even to a supermarket. They needn't be expensive, just attractive. Again, don't overdo it.

When I was a five, a friend of my mother's came for a visit. We knew that the family across the street was away for the summer. The octogenarian lady next door was ill. My mother's friend took me across the street to the beautiful flower garden and said, "It is too bad to let these flowers go to waste. Why don't we pick some and give them to Mrs. Van Ness to cheer her up?" We picked quite a bouquet and left them with Mrs. Van Ness's butler as a gift from me. A few days later, a large tin of cookies that her cook had made appeared at our door with a lovely note from the recovered Mrs. Van Ness. Before long she was back to her evening ritual of walking up and down the street, martini in hand, with her butler trailing her with the silver shaker.

Gardening is also a favorite pastime of old money. I am not advocating that you should cut your own lawn. However, working in the soil and watching plants grow can be very satisfying. Most just work with their gardener or landscape architect to plan the garden. Some do the actual weeding, wall building, and such, but many are content to prune the flowers and plan what grows well and where, remove what is not doing so well, etc.

On Cape Cod, Mr. and Mrs. Edwin Sibley Webster maintained a fabulous rose garden overlooking Quisset Harbor, which they opened to the public in 1930. It became so popular that they had to buy land across the road for parking. After Mrs. Webster's death in 1969, the garden and house were demolished. However, many people still talk about the Webster rose garden.

Similarly, Doris Duke maintained different gardens in greenhouses on her New Jersey farm, which were open to the public. After her death, oddly, there were no instructions regarding the property. The directors of her foundation wisely chose to open the grounds and restore the greenhouses for the public use.

Many gardens remain open to the public, thanks to the generosity of the millionaires who planted them. These include Longwood Gardens between Philadelphia and Wilmington, Winterthur in Wilmington, Biltmore in Asheville, North Carolina, the Asticou and Thuya Gardens in Northeast Harbor, Maine, and many others. You obviously do not have to do anything on the scale of these lovely places, but they are examples of the appreciation of beauty that the very rich have.

5

On Vacation

*M*any rich people own vacation homes. While traveling is fun, it is also good to have a base to get your children involved in sports like sailing, tennis, and golf with friends of their own sort. Often, these add balance to families' lives. If they are particularly busy in their hometown or city, they might choose the simplicity of a camp in the Adirondacks or a beach house so that they can feel the sand between their toes. Others prefer vacation homes where they are just as busy as at home. Think about this, though: a second or third house is an added responsibility. It is well worth it, however. And you can have the house and still travel. My sister always liked to spend a few weeks in the south of France and then go to her summer house in New England. It was only a few hours from their city house, so they used it on weekends well into the fall.

If you choose to buy a vacation house, think it out first. Do you favor the ocean or the mountains? Do you want a ranch in Wyoming, a camp in the Adirondacks, or a cottage on the beach? In the winter, do you like Florida or Arizona?

Would you like to spend part of the winter hunting on your plantation in the Low Country or on a golf course in Arizona or California? Or maybe you would prefer skiing in Park City or Aspen?

Probably, if you are social climbing, you do not favor the solitude of a ranch or plantation. Even a camp in the Adirondacks can be lonely unless you import friends. However, people love to visit vacation homes, so take that into account.

You might consider renting at first to see how you like the community and fit in socially. Some places are probably too closed to consider unless you are invited. These would be places like Wianno and Oyster Harbor (locals say "the Cape" when referring to these towns); Fishers Island (just called "Fishers"); Harbor Point, Michigan; and in Maine, Seal Harbor, Northeast Harbor ("Northeast"), and Isleboro. In Florida, don't try to bust into Hobe Sound (referred to as "Jupiter" or "Jupiter Island"). Most other towns are available for social climbers with enough money.

Before you pick a town, check out the local paper and any websites to see what kind of activities are available without joining a club. Hopefully you know some people who go to the town. Ask them about it. How they react to your queries will tell you how you will do there. If they are very encouraging, by all means go for it. However, don't make any assumptions. If they wince or look slightly ill, choose somewhere else. Many communities are built around clubs, especially in resorts. While these are not necessarily exclusive, they can be very nice and welcoming.

A friend of mine who lived in Tuxedo Park put his house on the market. The people who bought it assumed that membership in the Tuxedo Club came with the real estate. It did not. They did not gain membership in the club and moved elsewhere, losing quite a bit of money, as the real estate market had turned bad. So be sure of exactly *what* you are buying.

When I was growing up, Southampton and Palm Beach were meccas of old money—not so much anymore. As happens, much of the old money ran out, and new fortunes came in. Now both places are meccas for nouveau riche with a smattering of old money. Social climbers do very well in these two spots, but you may find yourself surrounded with other social climbers as the old money hides out.

Choose a town for the activities that interest you and your family. If you like skiing, don't go to Palm Beach just because social climbers do very well there. You would have a better time in Park City or Aspen. If you love the mountains, think about Vermont or the Rockies. Don't just go somewhere to social climb. While it is a full-time job, you do need to relax. And most good resorts are grist for the social mill.

The West is generally more open to nouveau riche than the East, although you will still have to follow the rules of society. Another way to check out a town is to stay in a local inn. There are many of these: from the Chatham Bars Inn on Cape Cod to the Gasparilla Inn in Boca Grande. You can meet some local people, see what kinds of activities are available locally, and determine how interested you are in coming back. If you find a place you think you will like, then rent there. If you and your family are at ease and making friends, you have found your new vacation home.

Follow the rules about buying your primary residence. Look for an old house in a good neighborhood. Get a well-respected architect and landscape designer. If you have formed a particularly good relationship with your decorator at home, by all means bring him or her in to do this job.

If not, most resorts have access to very good decorators. Remember that this is a vacation house, so decorate it accordingly. The days of the large Newport cottages are over. Give it a relaxed feeling in appropriate colors and fabrics. The decorator should have a handle on this. At a vacation house, it is not necessary to have sterling flatware or much silver. Rich people love to feel that they are relaxing and getting away from the cares of their primary house, even if the help does all the work there.

Only the truly rich need full-time staffs while on vacation. You can probably get by in most places with a cleaning woman (if you are a good cook and like doing it). A large house will need someone every day. If you do have full-time staff and wish to take them to your vacation house, be sure that there is plenty of room. You will probably be having many guests, so if you have a large house, they will come in handy.

If you are from a common background, you may want to limit the guests you have. Perhaps you have family members who have not shown the same social ambition as you. When they are visiting, perhaps it is best not to go to the club or local benefits with them. If they do not dress up to your standards, feel free to outfit them. You probably cannot go as far as to ask them to change their habits, however. If your brother-in-law likes to spend the day drinking beer and watching NASCAR, then he probably won't like going out on a boat to fish or going for a round of golf at the club.

A good way to social climb is to offer your vacation house for a few weeks to a local charity at home for an auction. This is also tax deductible. And often, when people sober up and realize what they have purchased, they will not get around to using it.

Remember, while you are not there, you will need a caretaker. Your local real-estate agent will be able to help out with suggestions on caretakers and where to go for various things. Consider this while you are looking for and purchasing your property. Your local real-estate agent can be invaluable also. The best can get you to clubs and introduce you around, if they feel you will be a good reflection on their business.

6

TRAVELING

A tour of the Continent or a trip around the world used to be part of a rich youth's education. It was a base on which he or she would place much of his or her cultural life. Rich people always spoke at least a second language, usually French, and always took Latin so they would have a basic knowledge of many romance languages. With the growth of globalism, more people are speaking more languages out of necessity rather than cultural curiosity.

It is also important to learn other cultures' customs. For instance, Americans switch the fork from the left hand to the right hand after cutting meat. In Europe, they leave it in the left hand, which really makes more sense. There are many subtleties in different countries. It is impolite to cut potatoes with a knife in Germany. Today, the world is certainly a more integrated place, so all cultures recognize their differences, but it is always wise and much appreciated to try to follow the local customs when possible.

People with money like to use it for travel. Some do it in their own planes or lease jets part time. (If you are going to do this, you can say it is for the comfort of the dog or that air travel has become such a chore.) Some go first class; others go coach. They travel everywhere and anywhere. Some like going back to the same places all the time. One couple I know goes to Paris every year for two or three weeks. Granted, they have been other places, but they are inordinately fond of Paris. When their daughters were growing up, there were all sorts of international programs for the girls to take part in. One loved sailing. Rather than just sail with the Northeast Harbor fleet, she spent most summers in high school sailing different places around the world with different groups. She also met interesting girls from other parts of the world, which exposed her to other cultures.

One couple I know reserves a hotel room the night before they arrive in Europe. That way, when they arrive in the morning they won't have to wait to get into their room.

Once, after one allegedly event-filled trip to Europe, my parents sailed home and had such a good time on the ship that they invited the captain home for the weekend. It must have been a fun trip because my mother and one of my father's friends bought a small car. ("What kind was it?" "I'm not sure." "What happened to it?" "I don't remember.") I asked what they did all weekend with the captain, but I got a very vague answer.

Their weekends with guests usually went this way: If the people arrived Friday night, there were cocktails and dinner and more cocktails at home. If they were family friends, the children ate with the adults. Saturday mornings, the guests usually slept in, and the parents might get up for some family time. Sometimes there was swimming, or they played tennis. Then there would be Bloody Marys and lunch either at home or at someone else's house. This usually wrapped up midafternoon, and people could read, nap, walk, or go about their own business. Then it was all hands on deck at five thirty or six o'clock for cocktails. Then there was usually either a dinner party at our house or someone else's. This would last far into the night. Sunday morning everyone in the family and whichever guests wished were off to church. After this, it was home for the papers and a sizable brunch. People were free to go home but usually lingered.

In the summer, most Sundays were spent at my grandmother's farm. She had taken a stone barn and had converted it to a large playhouse for the grandchildren and great-grandchildren, who ranged in age from midthirties to infants. It also gave her space if she was having more than thirty for lunch. Tables were set up here so the family could all be together. There were tennis courts and a spring-fed pond that she had cemented over to become a swimming pool. It was still spring-fed and had no filtering system, so it had to be emptied and cleaned every ten days or so, which kept it nice and bracingly chilly. And then there was the farm aspect, also, which we could explore to the farmers' irritation. At any rate, I am sure the captain was well-entertained.

After the Second World War, Americans acquired a reputation as loud and boorish while traveling, especially in Europe. When I was in college, my father thought it would be nice to take the family skiing in Austria for Christmas and New Year's. He had stopped in Paris to buy champagne for Christmas Eve and New Year's Eve. The inn where he took us was lovely, and most of the guests were pleasant. Although we were a large group, we were fairly well-behaved. However, there was one group who were very loud and coarse. They were not Americans and seemed to dislike everything about Americans. Finally, one morning after they threw a firecracker across the lobby, the management threw them out of the inn and arranged for them to be escorted across the border. For once, the Americans were not the black sheep.

Until fairly recently, traveling was just for the rich. Now the masses go abroad regularly. The trick is knowing where to go and when. You might want to get a Platinum American Express Card and read *Departures* magazine. It is full of good information. Also with this, a good travel agent will help. Perhaps for the novice, traveling in a group or on a tour is a good way to go. Abercrombie & Kent is one of several very well-respected agencies that set up guided travel arrangements. There are several reasons for traveling this way. First, the experience you will have will give you something to bring into discussions. You will see different places and learn different cultures. And if you are lucky, you will meet the people you aspire to be among. At any rate, A&K has many trips to select from, all of them interesting.

If you are traveling to Europe, you should go by boat at least once in your life. I'm not talking about one of those hideous cruise liners that hold thousands of people who spread their germs and where everyone wears sequins and comes down with either some dreaded stomach illness or food poisoning. It is slow and luxurious, and again, it will give you the chance to meet people. A nice smaller ship is what you want. The place to sit is at the captain's table, but mostly this is reserved for the very people you are aspiring to be with. I've never had to buy my way in, but it probably can be done. It depends how desperate you are.

Another good way to travel is with university and museum groups. They are usually centered on cultural or environmental tours, so this will help with your general education as well. An example of a National Geographic

Tour is a cruise to Alaska. The boat only holds 125. It is both intimate and educational.

You should learn at least most of the luxury hotels in the United States and Europe. You should learn a few others throughout the rest of the world. You should also learn some restaurants in major cities and what the highlights are in the United States and Europe. This will give you a good base for discussing or at least listening to discussions about travel and will give you good ideas of where you might enjoy going.

You should also study some geography and history. You can even do this online. If you hear of a place or event that takes your interest, just Google it. This will also work for many of the people you are striving to call friends. Just about anyone of import has some history on the Internet, whether they like it or not.

If you do not speak a foreign language, it is OK. If you want to acquire one, do so. Learn fairly fluently, or you will fail to impress and it will get you nowhere. Don't be like poor Olivia who said, "I can speak French: Chevrolay coupay parked on the highway," or who, on her first time in Paris at the Hotel Lotti said, "Chode, frode—which one's hot, and which one's cold?" It amused Uncle Tim—but no one else.

7

CHARITIES, VOLUNTEERING, AND COMMON

INTERESTS

Usually the old rich are very traditional. Men work, and the ladies do social things, hence, putting the weight of social life on female shoulders. The town where I grew up was noted for not being very welcoming to newcomers, which has changed. At the time, there were not many charities, but one way to get involved was through volunteering at the hospital, the Episcopal church's rummage sale (they still seem to have a lock on good rummage sales), or the small animal rescue league. (Old-moneyed people are inordinately fond of animals.) If there is a local museum, consider being a docent. This is still a good way to be accepted, ultimately, by society. Of course, cash donations are good, but you don't want to be too aggressive early on. Don't try to buy your way in.

Consider volunteering. There are many charities today, and every social climber should find at least a few interesting. If invited, attend fundraisers also. It is best if you are asked to sit at someone's table. That way you are not at the mercy of the seating committee. If they don't know you, they will probably put you with other outsiders, and that is not your goal, although they may be very nice people. And remember the woman who fled the benefit because she thought the table was not good enough. She is someone who people in at least three towns try to avoid.

If you play your cards right, you will be asked to be on a committee or a board or two. Be careful here. Committee work can be quite involved but fun. However, you may find that there is more involved than just buying some tickets and going to some meetings. Sometimes committees actually arrange the decorations, set up the tents, and do any other jobs so that the raised money can actually go to the charity. This, however, can be a great way to meet people and earn their friendship and respect.

If you are asked to be on a board, find out what is expected of you. Take the executive director and the president of the board to lunch. After a few pleasantries, get down to business and ask questions: How much will you be expected to raise or give? What kind of time commitment is involved? Be sure you are able to fulfill your obligations before you accept. Board work is not to be undertaken lightly. If you get on a board and do not pull your weight, word will get around. Sloughing off on charity work has felled many a social climber.

Another way to climb is through common interests, although, getting in garden clubs and book groups can be tricky; if asked, join. If you are a very good bridge player, usually there are bridge games, especially at resorts, which are open to the public.

Sports are also a good way to share an interest. However, never cheat, or that will be the end, and word will get around. Golf, tennis, paddle tennis, and other racket sports usually will have ladies' leagues in your town. Men might have to make a bit more of an effort finding the right group. If you get friendly with a few people, you can ask about joining a club. Make sure you pick the right club, though.

If you are a man and shoot trap and skeet, see about joining a local gun club. Good shots are always welcome. I belonged to a gun club where the best shooter was a self-made guy who was a little rough around the edges. I don't think he was particularly a social climber; he just liked to shoot. He ended up being invited around the world to hunt with members of the club and quite enjoyed himself.

If you need lessons in shooting or fishing, Orvis in Manchester, Vermont, is a very good source. All clubs have golf and tennis pros, but until you get into one, public tennis centers and some public golf courses have pros. You can also contact the pros at clubs to see about getting private lessons on the side. In all sports, it is appropriate to have the right attire, both for comfort and for style. The pros can coach you in this as well. However, it is the ladies who make the socializing decisions. So it is up to the social-climbing ladies to learn their way.

Rich people have a variety of pastimes, interests, and hobbies. These keep them occupied if they have time on their hands, or as an escape from the toils of their chosen careers. Collecting is a favorite pastime, and interests are varied among the rich: bibliophiles, jazz lovers, art collectors, etc. These interests can run from inexpensive to outrageous, but it is the interest that matters, not the expense. If you love walking the beach and collecting shells, when you have enough, display them. Get books about shells to identify them. Rich people love the simple things in life. If you are into horse racing, you don't have to own a stable, but a box at the track is a nice and a good way to entertain friends.

Other hobbies can be anything from needlework to the arts (painting, sculpting, writing, music) to reading. Anything you are interested in and enjoy doing can become a great pastime. Try a few things out. Once you get proficient, it will open other topics of conversation—although don't become a bore on the subjects.

Boats are another fascination for the rich. Some have two or three homes and a boat in every port, as it were. These also vary from small sailboats to large motor yachts. Often when people have a larger boat, they will transport it between their winter home and their summer home. That is fine if they are all on the same coast. There are many people who will have a home in the East, a home in the West, and maybe a home in a place like Harbor Springs, Michigan. They might have boats in all three, if they are passionate enough.

Some old money goes beyond extravagant in other ways. When Seward Johnson was building a $23 million house for his third wife in Princeton, he bought a farm nearby to live in temporarily. Among the changes he made to his temporary domicile was a ten-car garage with a barbershop that could be accessed by a tunnel from the house. Unfortunately, by the time the work was complete, he had eleven cars. The solution was simply to build another garage. The new house he was building had heated dog kennels attached to the master bedroom suite with ramps to the garden below and Baccarat crystal for panes in the kitchen cabinets. It is now a golf club.

Antique cars also seem to fascinate people with money. They will either have one or two they leave at one of their homes for an amusing spin around town, or they will collect them. Often, the wealthy will be so passionate about collecting that they will set up their own museum. In Sandwich, Massachusetts, Josiah K. Lilly III had inherited so many collections and formed so many of his own collections that he set up the Heritage Museum and Gardens. It houses military miniatures, stamps, eighteenth-century paintings, American folk art, and the J. K. Lilly III automobile museum, housed in a Shaker barn.

In Shelburne, Vermont, on the shores of Lake Champlain, Electra Havemeyer Webb founded the Shelburne Museum with her collections. There are seventeenth- through twentieth-century artifacts, nineteenth-century folk art, and nineteenth- and twentieth-century decoys and carriages all housed in eighteenth- and nineteenth-century buildings brought from around New England. There is also the steamship *Ticonderoga* that used to cruise Lake Champlain. All of this was the interest of Mrs. Webb, and she left it all to the public. The interior of her New York apartment was moved to the museum after her death.

These are just two of many very rich people who took their hobbies to an extreme. They had generations of money behind them. As a social climber, you will want to start out smaller, even if you have a couple billion dollars. Pick a subject you find interesting enough to study or a pastime you love. Become proficient enough to be considered a minor authority on it, and you may impress people and surprise yourself. However, as a social climber, make sure that it has a wide enough audience who will care. I wouldn't recommend capturing African butterflies or taxidermy. I only mention that because once I knew such a couple. The wife had inherited pots of money. The family considered the husband beneath her, and he was many years younger. If he saw a dead animal by the side of the road, he would pick it up, have it stuffed, and present it to his wife. She actually loved them. I'm not sure if any other woman would feel the same.

The rich used to go big game hunting around the world and hang their trophies at home. This has pretty much gone out of favor, as more people are concerned about the environment and animal welfare. However, a photographic safari is another idea you might consider. If you are any good at photography, this could open many doors.

What is important is to develop more interests than just social climbing. You have to have some interests that will make you attractive to people.

8

MARRYING UP

*O*ne way to make it socially is to find a partner who is there already. This is done all too often. In the worst cases, it ends badly. Dominick Dunne related one of these tragedies in *The Two Mrs. Grenvilles*. Although society frowns on it, in the late eighteen hundreds and early nineteen hundreds, many wealthy families used their money to acquire titles. Perhaps the most famous was Consuelo Vanderbilt. Her mother broke up her true romance to force her into marriage to the Duke of Marlborough, who needed the fortune that accompanied his bride. Her mother, Alva Vanderbilt, was the most aggressive social climber of her time. In marrying her only daughter off, she gained bragging rights to having a duke for a son-in-law. It did not matter to her that her daughter was very much in love with someone else who was her social equal, though an American and untitled. Nor did it matter that her daughter was extremely unhappy and that her marriage, like Alva's, would end in divorce.

Sometimes, when it doesn't work out socially, it works out well anyway. There was a woman my family was acquainted with who was mistress to the scion of one of the country's great fortunes—and an only child. He was somewhat of a drinker and once tried to drive to Europe. He didn't make it very far. Although his drinking caused many health problems, he kept a mistress at one end of town. It was the 1930s, and he had never married, but when she somehow found herself with child, he did the honorable thing and married her. His family and society friends were shocked and refused her admittance to their drawing rooms. The story goes: hurt, she flew west for a vacation. He had a heart condition and could not go. While there, she called him and pleaded with him. He must fly out; she missed him very much. He had a heart attack on the plane and died. She inherited his vast fortune. Because she was not welcome to go out into society, she put herself to managing his money, which she did very well. Eventually, she was one of the wealthiest women in America. She went wherever she pleased, including the White House, to be honored for her work entertaining soldiers. She never let society's snub bother her, at least publicly, and she was very happy with her accomplishments. After the last of her husband's generation went to the big vault in the sky, the local gentry more and more accepted her.

If you are planning the actual wedding, there are some things you may want to take into account. While you may be loved by your intended and even by his or her family (or at least accepted by them), your family is a different matter, even for a few days during the actual wedding. Some friends had one child, a daughter. She had been raised with every advantage that money could buy. She had attended the best schools, had taken wonderful trips, and was very sophisticated. On top of being lovely, she was exceptionally smart and worked her way up quickly in the world of finance. She was approaching the end of her twenties and had been engaged twice, but it had not worked out. As I say, she was charming, beautiful, and smart, which was too much of a good thing for some men to handle. However, she did meet someone who had been a minor professional athlete before being sidelined by an injury. He worked in the same firm as she but was not the rising star that she was. However, they fell for each other. Her parents, realizing that she was getting beyond eligible age, were thrilled. They showered everything on the young man. Her mother had planned her wedding since she was a little girl, and it was to be fabulous. The two families spoke on the phone but never actually met. When the groom's family arrived, they did so in a pickup truck and a camper, missing only the grandmother in a rocking chair. They parked the camper at the groom's house, where the bride had put all her belongings before moving home for the wedding. At the rehearsal dinner, which the bride's family threw at their club, the groom's mother and sisters arrived wearing the bride's clothes, having raided her closet. The bride and her mother gasped but held their own. If only the ladies had raided the closet for the wedding. Their arrival was right out of *L'il Abner.* All they needed was some straw in their hair. The reception was not the most comfortable I have ever attended. The bride's side needed extra fortification from the bar; the groom's family frowned on drinking. The marriage itself did not fare much better. It turned out that the groom had a gambling addiction and a wandering eye. Three years later, the marriage went down in flames.

Not all marriages between classes are so doomed. However, unless your family is capable of fitting in or is at least prepared for the event, to avoid excruciating embarrassment, think about eloping or having a very small family wedding.

Be forewarned: marrying old money is no bed of roses if you are not used to it. It isn't all shopping and having people wait on you. There are social and societal demands that, if you are unprepared, can eat away at your happiness. Obviously, the responsibilities are not those of marrying into the royal family, but they can seem as such. The saying goes: "To whom much is given, much will be required." If you are prepared, it will not be easy, but it will be a lot smoother. Probably there will be some charity work expected. Your behavior will be scrutinized either openly or silently. People will be waiting for you to make a mistake—don't. Sometimes, people can treat others whom they don't consider their equals with condescension. Just remember, if they do, they are the ones lacking manners. Condescension is never called for or appreciated. Just ignore them and respond politely. They were probably in your shoes once.

Just remember who you are and what you want out of life. Don't weaken. Do not turn to drugs or alcohol, which often happens with dreams that do not come true. There are many rehab facilities that are filled with both old money and new who could not bear the strain. They are not, however, the most reliable places to meet a spouse.

Old-moneyed families are very strong and can overwhelm you. Hold your own if that is the way you choose to go. Unless you are tricking someone into marriage, which is not a good idea, be clear ahead of time with him or her that you are not just friends and lovers but allies against the world, perhaps starting with the family. If you feel overwhelmed by the family, educate yourself in anything. It is a good escape. Learn what will make them respect—if not like—you. Ultimately, old money highly values loyalty. They are suspicious of you because they feel you will not make their child happy. If you can prove them wrong here, it is the best way to deal with it.

While old money may overlook or even be amused by one of their own being a drunk for a while—the guy who tried to drive to Europe—they don't care for outsiders perpetually making messes of themselves. There still seems to be a gender gap here, too. Women drunks are far less tolerated than men, unless the men become abusive either physically or emotionally.

Of course, the other side of marriage is divorce. During quite a contentious divorce, some friends of mine were going through valuations of their three houses. When the husband went to the house on Cape Cod to meet the appraiser, the caretaker met him and said how sorry he was about the marriage breaking up. The response was, "That makes one of us. It will be the happiest day of my life." Again, money cannot buy happiness. Although it cost him plenty financially, emotionally, and socially (as the wives hang together in times like this), he has been happy ever since.

Divorce, of course, can lead to a second marriage. Often, when money and children are concerned, things can go very badly. Uncle Tim used to refer to Olivia as EOS, for evil old stepmother. And he said it only half joking. She had wrecked his first marriage, had estranged his family, and had lost him his job and ultimately many of his friends, but she had seemed to make him happy. Not all cases are like this, but the author of *Cinderella* didn't come up with the EOS out of the blue! If you do decide to be a second or third wife, it will make for better familial relations and a happier life if you get along with the children and even the ex-wife of your intended. A friend in London had lunch with his first daughter-in-law. They were discussing her children, his grandchildren, and their stepmother. Daughter-in-law said,

"My children have the best of both worlds. We all get along smashingly well." It may take some effort at first, but as a social climber, you will need all the allies you can get.

Abuse is beyond a cardinal sin. If you marry up and find that you are the victim of abuse, get out. It will not stop. It will not go away. And no amount of money or social position is worth it. Do not be afraid to get help. Brooke Astor was first married to Dryden Kuser, who, by her own account, was a drunk and abusive. Although they had a child, she could not abide it and left him. She ultimately found happiness not once but twice, so don't be afraid your life is over.

9

You Can't Get Away with It

*T*here are some things social climbers should never try, and some they should definitely try to avoid. The rich are eccentric. All others are considered weird or mad as a hatter.

I had a friend, Jack, who had a farm with a large house, tennis court, pool, etc. He was a young bachelor and had lots of house parties for his college friends, their girlfriends, and eventually, their wives. One of his friends, Max, lived in Richmond, where he met a dancer in a men's bar. He asked to bring her one weekend. Jack, who was one of the most easygoing people ever, refused. An argument ensued, which led to Jack accepting the dancer. All others were forewarned, but because they liked Jack, because they knew Max was a bit eccentric, and mostly because they had known each other so long, all attended. It did not ruin the weekend, but the dancer never returned. She and Max eventually broke up, and he moved to Florida. You can't replace old friends.

Uncle Tim used to take Pat and some of his friends to "21" for lunch to celebrate Pat's December birthday, which was the day before his. (By this time, Granny had gone on to greener pastures, and Tim was back in the family business.) For Pat's fifteenth birthday a replica of one of the family corporation's deliver trucks was hung over their usual table, number thirty-two in the bar. The children would then go off to see a show, and the adults would do a little shopping and mostly a lot of drinking. One time, the children were sent off, and unfortunately, the adults did not go shopping. Around Christmastime, the Salvation Army band used to come into "21" and play carols for donations. Again, it was Olivia. She, having had too many cocktails, got up and sang the carols along with the band. At best, she had a voice that sounded like she had sandpaper in her larynx. Fortunately, due to Tim's position and friendship with the then owners, they were not tossed out. Oddly enough, the show the children went to see was *It's a Mad, Mad, Mad, Mad World*.

When I was growing up, a very social New York decorator came to visit my parents for the weekend. My parents had a dinner party. Dessert was blueberries with crème fraiche. After a bit too much wine, the decorator turned to the person next to her and said, "Don't you think they'd serve the peas with the main course?" The reply was, "I believe they are blueberries." "Oh," she answered and then reached for the crème fraiche but grabbed the tartar sauce that inexplicably had not been removed and ladled it on her berries. She seemed to quite enjoy them. The next morning she got up for breakfast bright and cheery. She got a cup of coffee, went to the bar, poured in some vodka, stirred it with the arm of her dark glasses, and was ready to face a new day.

A lady whose husband was head of a major New York museum at the time decided that a very valuable picture in their New York house would look fabulous over the sofa in the living room of their country house, which she was having redone. With the help of the housekeeper, she secured the large painting to the roof of her station wagon. All was well until she was in the Lincoln Tunnel. The picture flew off the roof, into the path of traffic behind. She stopped, as did the traffic, but not until several cars and trucks had driven over the painting. All was well, as it went to the museum for restoration and does indeed look terrific.

People with old money seem to be comfortable making gaffes, knowing that their friends will excuse them. Once I was at a dinner party, and one of the guests seemed to be related—or his wife was related—to half of Philadelphia. For some reason during cocktails, he thought it would be fine to just pick up a wing chair and march it across the room. In putting it down, he cracked the leg. He, however, did not notice. The hostess said nothing to anyone and prayed that his considerable bulk would not crash the chair to the ground. It did not. He went into dinner and then into coffee without knowing. The chair was sent out and repaired. If a social climber had done the same thing, it might not have gone so smoothly in the end.

The man who tried to drive to Europe was a next-door neighbor of my grandmother. He would pay a formal call several times a year. He, however, was incontinent. My grandmother would have a towel placed on the chair where he was to sit. He would pay his call, and if he had an accident, the towel was put in the laundry after he left. It's amazing what people will do for old friends and old money.

Another fellow I know, who is one of the waspiest wasps ever, eats almost everything, including pizza and sandwiches, with a knife and fork. He simply does not want to touch his food with his hands. On the other end of the spectrum, I have seen one gentleman actually lick his paper plate after a picnic. He was a known eccentric, so no one took notice.

My mother had a friend who was extremely wealthy. Her lawyer's firm paid her bills. As a hobby she bought houses she liked and had a very pricy architect fix them up. Then she would either rent them out or leave them empty so she could visit. She lived in a three-bedroom ranch house herself. She bought most of her clothes at Kmart. She really resembled a bag lady. Once she went into a local decorator, looking for a table, and was ignored. She went down the street. That decorator did get her a table—for $27,000. She knew my mother favored Norman Norell. Once she came back from New York and announced that she had bought a Norell sable coat. It went well—even with Kmart!

And then there was the New York socialite in the 1920s, who had her two Russian wolfhounds as her bridesmaids. No one blinked an eye, but no one ever forgot it either. She remained quite eccentric her whole life and was really quite charming.

One question that is unfortunate from anyone at any occasion—unless you run into them in a foreign city—is "What are you doing here?" If they are asking, it is clearly not their event or party. Therefore, it is not their business who invited you. There really is no answer. It is such a rude question that all you can say is "There really is no answer to that question; it is so rude."

One thing no one can get away with is chasing another person's spouse. It happens all the time in every town, and unless the two are willing to face the consequences, it never ends well. There are stories of wealthy men seducing and marrying their wives' maids, but it doesn't happen often. Usually it ends with someone in disgrace. And the stories never die; they just fade. Once a friend of mine was in a conversation about the very old gossip in town. The other person said, "Who was Jonesy Moncrieff having that affair with back then?" He replied unashamedly, "That was my mother."

10

NAME-DROPPING, BRAGGING, BIGOTRY, AND GOSSIP

*T*here really is no point in name-dropping. People don't care who you know, and they really don't care what family a person belongs to. Just because someone is a member of a prominent family doesn't give him or her any magic powers or even insure that he or she is very interesting. If all that the individual has in his or her favor is whom he or she is related to, then that person probably isn't worth the time. And people usually don't like being branded by their family name or relation. That, too, can be a burden. Probably, though, it is the people who are branding that are shallow. If they think that is why the person is important, then they, too, are social climbers. People like to be recognized for themselves and whatever accomplishments they have made.

Sure, people who grew up together and all know each other will use names of friends freely. Don't fall into the trap, though. It is uncomfortable to drop names and have someone turn to someone else and say, "Do I know them?"

And it is quite rude to drop a well-known name unless you are sure that everyone knows the person.

No matter how proud you are of something, do not brag about it. That is for teenagers. If others wish to offer comments, that's fine. If it is a birthday or Christmas present, it is all right to say, "Look at this beautiful ring Oscar gave me." But unless you are planning to pass whatever it is along, they really don't care. It is like dragging out the album of your latest trip during a dinner party—just don't.

If someone else is guilty of bragging, don't try to one-up them. It never works, and it will take whatever wind is in their silly sails away. Just let them enjoy thinking that they are impressing people.

There was a time when bigotry was part of society. There were towns that had Christian country clubs and Jewish country clubs. In Palm Beach there were two very rich people who married. One was Christian, and one was Jewish. They could not go to each other's clubs. That seems ridiculous now, but there is still quite a bit of bigotry around. A friend was visiting at a family compound on the Rhode Island coast. While there, a cousin of the hostess had a dinner party. The cousin's parents were visiting. When my friend was introduced to her father, Uncle Bertram, Bertram said, "Oh, Irish." My friend was indeed of Irish descent, four generations ago. Then Bertram proceeded to say what good Irish maids he grew up with and whatnot. After a few minutes of such boorishness, he rattled the ice in his empty glass and said," Time to get more gin. Mother's milk to you people." My friend was shocked speechless. He reported it to another houseguest, who went into gales of laughter. She then told him their hostess's father despised Uncle Bertram and had feigned illness to avoid the dinner party. Bertram was a failure in business, had lost a lot of money, and was very bitter, hence taking his anger out on the world.

When my cousin was in grade school, one of his classmates was having people over to play. However, he could not have my cousin and a few others because they were Catholic, and his father did not want little Harry playing with Catholics. I don't know if the father was afraid that they would try to convert his little man or what. A few years later, the father purchased one of my family's businesses. He paid a lot more than he would have if he hadn't been mean to my cousin. A few decades after that, the father was head of a nonprofit. He had the nerve to apply for a grant from my family's foundation. The same cousin was president of the foundation. I forget what the nonprofit was or if they got their grant, but knowing the head of it was a bigot did not help things. Be very careful whom you offend.

Don't fall into the bigotry trap. Bigotry is really just a way for insecure people to feel better about themselves. If you are around bigotry, don't join in. Loudmouth bigots usually just end up causing embarrassment all around. And beware: the person with whom you are speaking has all kinds of relatives by marriage. If you make a comment about a race or religion, it will be noted and remembered. You cannot take back words after they have left your mouth, no matter how many apologies you attempt to make.

Gossip is merely talking about someone else's private business and affairs. It is certainly a part of everyone's life, whether they admit it or not. And it is not necessarily always idle or malicious. If someone is ill, people take them food; or worse, if someone dies, friends help out the family. To discuss these matters is gossip, but it is also kindness. It is certainly justifiable and even praiseworthy.

However, really juicy gossip is probably not so kind or charitable. Although it, too, is always a part of everyday life, you have to be careful here. First, assume that when you say something that can be construed to be negative about someone, he or she will hear what you said. People love to get the rumor—or worse, innuendo—back to the subject. Then the subject has to deny it, which is difficult; once enough people have heard the tale, it is believed to be true. Or the subject can call on you to rescind the offense. If it is indeed untrue, this is really your only honorable choice. This puts you in the awkward and humiliating position of admitting that you lied or at least said something that you had not verified, which will put everything you say in question and damage whatever trust people have in you. At any rate, people will eventually find the truth themselves, and if you have spread vicious, untrue rumors, it will certainly come back to haunt you.

Then there is idle gossip, which is neither praiseworthy nor harmful. It is just everyday bits of useless information, such as so-and-so had a facelift, or she didn't pay the slip-cover man. It is stored away to be dragged out later. It may have a slight dig to it, but nothing fatal. People seem to like idle gossip, especially about those who are not at the top of the popularity list.

What you need to be careful of is truly malicious gossip. If you meet someone who is always saying nasty and potentially harmful things about other people, be wary of them. I can assure you, everyone else is. And who knows what they are saying about you? These people either are bitter about the turn their own lives took and are out to make sure others suffer as well, or they are social climbers who never made it as far as they wished, and they are still trying in the only way that they feel is left to them. It is no way to get ahead. Destroying other people's reputations is a serious matter. It is perhaps the vilest of pastimes. Do not ever fall into this trap. If you do not make it as a social climber, accept it. This kind of person always ends up a true social pariah.

11

How to (and How Not to) Dress

Today, the country seems to be going through a sartorial breakdown. It is not all right to wear workout clothing anywhere but while working out. People do not want to see other people's perspiring armpits—or worse. There was a day when there were rules on how to dress. Those rules seem to be largely forgotten. It is fine to dress comfortably but with a modicum of good taste. Even Aunt Olivia was fairly well dressed most of the time—thanks to Bergdorf's. If you have doubts, go to a high-end store like Bergdorf Goodman or Paul Stuart and get sound advice from the salespeople. They are usually very reliable and discreet. Remember the saleswoman in *Pretty Woman*. She was based on some very real people, who are available to help you dress with confidence.

It is all right to have a small logo on a polo shirt or even a shirt, but if something is emblazoned on the shirt, advertising the maker, forget about it. These are made for the throngs who spend their Sundays at the outlet malls.

Keep your hairstyle classic and simple. Ladies should go to a terrific salon to have their hair styled. Men should get a good haircut—short and simple. Facial hair is discouraged.

Remember, there is a big difference between fashion and style. Don't just be fashionable; be stylish. If you look at something that you think is ridiculous, it probably is. Just because someone wore it to the Oscars or to the Grammys doesn't mean it is going to look good on you. Chances are, it didn't look good on them either, and they may not have even owned it. Perhaps you should study the way stylish people dressed throughout the ages. Don't copy them. Just study them to get an idea of style. People like the Duke and Duchess of Windsor—she was a very successful social climber—or Brooke Astor, who reigned as the queen of New York, had a style of their own. Most people would look a bit ridiculously overdressed dressed as they were. However, they dressed for their parts. Unless you are a former king and his notorious wife or a living legend, keep it simple.

There are certain things old-moneyed people have always had and, being who they are, will always have. One is the Vuitton logo. Nowadays, knockoffs of this can bought relatively inexpensively on the corner in many cities. Let's face it: most women have a version of it. It is not particularly chic anymore, but old money is not trying to be particularly fashionable, just stylish—remember? If you see a Vuitton bag in the grocery store, the woman can be an heiress or a secretary. However, if you see an Hermes bag in the grocery store, chances are that she is an heiress.

Long evening gloves have gone out of fashion unless you are a debutante or at some extremely formal party.

Men in black tie should usually wear a traditional tuxedo. All these Hollywood interpretations are unusual, and that is about it. They are not attractive or stylish. Black tie means black tie, not black shirt, not black sneakers, and certainly not white tie. There is a time and place for white tie. If that is called for, fine. But black tie means only that. In summer, or at a resort, a white dinner jacket may be substituted for the black jacket. On a social climber, this can look a bit stilted. Also, tie and cummerbund combinations that are anything but black should be left to old money—the simpler, the better. Be sure to wear studs and cufflinks instead of buttons. While it may sound dull, ladies still think it is the most elegant suit a man can wear. The one place you may take liberties is with your shoes. Unless you are going to a ball, where dancing pumps are de rigueur, you can wear any black shoes; even fancier are Stubbs & Wooten slippers or some other needlepoint slippers (black background). But again, the more conservative, the better; don't look the fop.

Another item many old-moneyed men wear is the signet or crest ring. There was a time when these were stylish. Now most jewelry on men seems a bit garish. However, if it was a graduation gift from your grandmother, who was proud that you were carrying on the family tradition and were a third or fourth generation to graduate from Princeton, then it is all right.

In the whole matter of jewelry, men need to be careful. Absolutely no gold chains anytime, anywhere. If you have a medical condition, you can wear a Medic Alert bracelet (preferably gold from Tiffany's). A good Swiss watch is a must. My family favors Patek Philipe or Vacheron Constantin, but there are many. Cuff links are acceptable as are studs and cuff links with a tuxedo. Any ring but a wedding ring is questionable, even if you won the Super Bowl. For social climbers, less is better here.

Ladies should also be careful not to get too carried away. Remember that you will be moving about in your frock, so until you are practiced, don't get too carried away with trains, flounces, etc. And certainly don't reveal too much cleavage. It will not win points with other ladies, and they are the social rulers. A good salesperson can tell you what is simple but elegant. I repeat: don't overdress or overaccessorize.

Daytime clothing is another area where standards have fallen for both men and women. When did people start thinking it was all right that if you were walking around Manhattan, you could dress as if you were going to Coney Island? I remember once, when living in Manhattan, going to the doctor. It was a crisp fall day. I thought I was pretty nattily dressed in corduroys, Gucci shoes, and a cashmere sweater. The first thing the doctor said was "My, aren't we casual today?"

If in doubt, ladies, in summer, can go with Lillys and Belgian shoes or sandals until they get their confidence. In winter, stick with a line like Carlisle, which is always tasteful, or a good classic designer. You can work your way up from there. See the appendix "Accoutrements for Social Climbers" for any items that you may need. And go easy on the makeup. It is supposed to enhance your features, not make you look like a streetwalker. Maybe get professional help here as well.

For men, while it is no longer necessary to wear a tie and jacket every day or even while traveling, it is necessary to look neat, tidy, and well dressed. Blue jeans have become acceptable for touring. With proper shoes, a collared shirt, and maybe a sweater or jacket, they are acceptable. If, however, you are going to a nice restaurant or even on a shopping expedition, dress up a bit. Just remember: traveling is not an occasion to wear something resembling your pajamas. Wear what makes you comfortable without looking like you are about to change the oil in your pickup truck. And if you must wear a cap, make sure the bill faces front and that you remove it indoors or at meals. Caps are becoming all too prevalent in all levels of society. Unless you are bald, think about leaving the cap in the closet.

As for athletic wear, keep it for the gym or other exercise venues. It is all right to do an errand or two en route to exercising. However, do not linger all day in them. And for that matter, men should avoid "wife-beater" shirts. No one wants to see your underarm hair. And unless you are in a swim meet, no Speedos.

One last note that I hope is unnecessary. If you have any tattoos, have them removed—immediately.

12

Dinner Conversation and Entertaining

*I*t is very important to learn the art of dinner conversation. First, never ask, "What do you do?" A friend of mine had a standard answer: "I have my own business, and I mind it." Actually, people's occupations are a very middle-class concern. These people don't care what you do as long as you don't end up behind bars. They care who you are and how you behave. They are much more interested in your interests and pastimes. And don't try to impress them. It will only bore them. Also, know when to keep quiet. If the conversation gets out of your comfort zone, just listen and agree politely.

It is, of course, best if you know a bit about the other guests or, at least, your dinner partners. A friend of mine was head of a large New York business, and his business involved a lot of dinners where he and his wife would meet total strangers. When the car would pick up his wife to go to dinner, on the seat would be a little dossier on the people that they would be dining with so that she could ask informed questions and make polite conversation.

This, unfortunately, cannot be done in everyday life. If you know nothing about your dinner partner, keep it simple. Religion and politics used to be off-limits for public discussion. They probably still should be, but all too often they, particularly politics, are brought up. Avoid the discussion. These topics are way too personal and controversial for polite conversation. The weather is too shallow a topic. Simply say, "So, tell me about yourself." That leaves people open to divulge as much or as little as they wish, and people usually like to talk about themselves. Pay attention and remember what you are told. People really appreciate it when you meet them again and remember what they told you.

Money is another topic that you need to avoid, unless it is about the economy or some other general topic. Never discuss how much money you have or what you earn. The only time people's money is a topic of conversation is if they have lost it. Then it is only mentioned quietly in sympathetic tones because they are selling their house or are posted at the club for nonpayment of their bill.

Just remember: it is a conversation, not an interview. Don't ask too many personal questions. I know one lady who was seated at a dinner party between two men who did not know each other. After she had spoken to the man on her right for a few minutes, she was speaking with the man on her left, who was a friend. Instead of speaking to his other dinner partner, the man on her right joined their conversation. He asked the other man such questions as "What is your line of business?" "Telecommunications." Which brought the query "Where?" The questions just were not going to stop. So, after a few questions, the lady jumped in and said, "He's the chairman of AT&T. Anything else you want to know?"

People like to talk about themselves but grow uncomfortable being given the third degree. And think before you speak. Don't sound like an airhead. You don't have to discuss Dostoevsky, but the latest issue of *People* magazine isn't good either.

If possible, establish a common connection. On one occasion, I was seated next to an older lady whom I had heard was a real snob, and I also discovered that she had atrocious breath. She was quite cool, as I expected. And then I saw her studying my place card. She brightened noticeably and asked if I was related to Mary Kerney. "Yes," I said, "she is my aunt." Well, they had gone to the local school for girls together about a century before, but it established me as being OK with her. Her behavior was not praiseworthy. If she had had good manners, she would have been polite to begin with, no matter who I was. However, I knew that her family had lost their money in the Great Depression. She and her brother had both married people with pots of money, but they always remained insecure, and thus useless, bitter snobs with no reason to be snobs at all. They should have been grateful for what they had—or at least for whom they had married.

Another time, I was at a large dinner party with many tables. One of my dinner partners was a society girl who had married a scion to one of the country's great media fortunes. On her other side was someone who was self-made and a bit rough around the edges. She was extremely condescending to him throughout the main course. Then she actually moved to another table for dessert. The hostess, quite a good friend of mine, came along and was quietly furious. I doubt the society girl was invited back. Her marriage later broke up for different reasons.

When you are entertaining, there are some things to do and some things definitely to avoid. If you don't have help, plan a meal that lets you remain with your guests. It should be the company—as much as the food—that people enjoy. It avoids confusion if you use place cards for a dinner. If there is a guest of honor, he should be placed on the hostess's right, or she should be on the host's right. Do not place couples next to each other. They see each other enough. If there are two people who don't know each other but you think would enjoy each other, seat them near each other. Make sure the dinner conversation remains lively, without turning brash. If the conversation turns in a direction that may lead to trouble, steer it elsewhere.

Remember: people come to your house either because they like you or want to get to know you better, so just be yourself. If not everyone leaves thinking that you are wonderful, that is all right. However, be sure not to stint on the food and liquor. If you are a great cook, it is all the better. People always like to eat where they know the food is good. And do not try to get by with cheap liquor or wine. Old money can't, though many try. It just looks cheap. And if you are currently used to drinking cheap sweet wine or sweet mixed drinks, grow up. You are not in college anymore. Learn to like good wine and grown-up drinks.

Once I went to a dinner party that should have been a hit. The setting was lovely; the food was delicious. However, I should have been suspicious when a lady friend came over and said, "I must talk to you now because I won't have the chance at dinner." When it came time to sit, there were two tables of eight. The men were directed to one, and the ladies to another. It was a frightful bore. Then about eight thirty, the hostess stood up and said it was time to go to bed. Everyone was rather relieved to leave. It was really a waste of a nice evening.

It is usually best, particularly when you are new to the game, to have a standard party. If the guests are interesting, the food wonderful, and the liquor top-notch, then it is bound to be a good party. You don't need any gimmicks. Later, when you are a bit surer of your footing socially, you might mix it up a bit.

13

YOU ARE WHAT YOU EAT

*W*hile they may stop at McDonalds when driving the family and the dogs to Maine or Florida, the rich do not make a habit of fast-food restaurants. There are certain staples they favor (list appended). A favorite is the BLT. You can count on old money ordering a BLT or a club sandwich if they are hungry. And deviled eggs are another favorite.

Their taste buds are developed as they grow up. Not every child likes lobster, asparagus, caviar, and turtle soup with sherry or even pâté. However, over time they develop a sophisticated palate at their parents' table as they learn table manners. Of course, they make faces and try not to eat some things. I remember as a child being served spaghetti with tomato sauce. It was rather exotic (at least at our table) in the 1950s. I said that I did not want to eat it. My father persevered, and I ate it. I then went into the servants' bathroom and got sick. We did not have spaghetti again for some time.

The rich are passionate about their food. Really old money used to like it bland. Slowly over time, palates have become more discerning. My father was ahead of his time. He played polo, tennis, and golf, shot skeet and trap, hunted birds and deer, went salmon and deep-sea fishing, and read an average of a book a night, but his passion was cooking and wine. When my parents moved into a larger house in the mid-1940s, his mother's house present was a Garland restaurant stove. He had a room built in the cellar to house his wine. It was always a treat to accompany him down as he unlocked the door and chose a few bottles.

We had a cook for every day, but if my father was cooking, it was an occasion. He did most of the cooking—or at least most of the preparation—when they entertained, and he always drew lots of compliments. He loved to go to France and bring back recipes, which was also an exotic thing to do in the 1940s and '50s. One thing he couldn't master was Maxim's apple pie, now known as tarte tatin. To make it worse, the cook made it perfectly. She did most of the baking in the house. She said that the only thing she did differently was to line up the apples in rows. My father was not patient enough to do that. He could be very patient for more complicated dishes. He made wonderful cassoulet. It took days to prepare, but it was delicious. He was famous among his crowd for many things but most of all for his cooking. Over time he gave up polo and tennis, fishing, and even shooting, but he always was a great cook.

While the rich have gotten more health conscious in modern times, they still appreciate the food they grew to like as children. While some of it is healthy enough, not all of it is. So it is a special treat if they get foie gras or tournedos rossini. They might make polite protestations to please their spouse, but who doesn't love béarnaise sauce or brownies? In their hearts, the rich would all like to be Julia Child or at least have her in the kitchen.

The rich also have their own family traditions as far as food goes. One family I knew liked to have smoked salmon topped with caviar on Christmas Day. It was over-the-top, but after all, it was Christmas. In the South, on a plantation, you are apt to get overfed, as the days are spent outdoors (or supposed to be). Breakfast might be pancakes or eggs, grits, bacon, sausage, biscuits, toast or muffins, fresh fruit and juice, and an assortment of cereals. Lunch might be deviled eggs, cheese and crackers, crudités and dip, wine, beer, and assorted soft drinks, quail, salad, potato salad, brownies, and cookies. Dinner, after cocktails and hors d'oeuvres, would be venison or fried chicken, potatoes, biscuits, a vegetable, salad, and dessert. Aside from these, there might be a bar with potato chips or pretzels, candies (peanut M&Ms are a favorite), and nuts for anytime snacking.

One thing that is proper is eating asparagus with your hands and even picking up chops. However, until you are more accepted, try to avoid it. It is fine to eat artichokes, shrimp, and other obvious things with your hands.

14

The Rich Do Economize

No matter how much money people have, there are savings to be had. Old money just doesn't waste money. Often the mode of saving is just an eccentricity, but almost every rich person has one. There was a couple that liked to spend the month of June in Beaulieu in the south of France. For a few years, they would stop over in Paris because they loved it. However, when Paris got very expensive, they decided to economize and skip that leg of the trip. Fortunately, they still went first class.

It is amazing how many rich people shop at warehouse stores, especially Costco and Walmart. A hundred saved is a hundred earned. And let's face it, the wines and packaged goods are the same. At Costco the meats and vegetables are very good, and if you have a family and a staff to feed, it makes sense. *Town & Country* even had a feature on how to give a cocktail party from Costco. And many rich people shop at outlets of better brands. But at outlets you have to tell which are the real deals and which are made specifically for the outlets.

Once I was on the board of a charity. Before one meeting started, the chair of the board, who was known as a local character, got up and announced that his daughter was going to go to Paris the next week but had to postpone her trip. Her ticket was nonrefundable, and he wondered if anyone was interested in buying it. The guy could have afforded to take the whole board to Paris for a month, but he did not want to lose the money on his daughter's ticket.

My sister bought a large summer house many years back. When I went to visit, I didn't recognize the monogram on the sheets and blanket covers. Thinking that she had inherited them from some unknown relative, I asked. It turned out that they had come with the house, and with ten bedrooms to outfit, it made sense to keep them. Would I have felt better if they had been Great Aunt Susie's? After all, they were laundered. She had redone most of the house, including a new kitchen and bathrooms—but new sheets and blanket covers would break the bank? She did bring her old monogrammed towels from her city house and got new ones there.

A friend of my parents' housekeeper worked for the family of a pharmaceutical heir. One of the sons had a summer job and would make his lunch every day to take to work. Once she said, "Billy, with your money, why don't you just buy lunch?" His reply was "Lizzie, that's why we have money." I don't think he meant it literally. After all, they are each worth billions. What he did mean was that they did not spend money carelessly.

A fellow I know not only inherited a sizable fortune from his parents but also their farm in Bucks County and their house on the Maine coast. Rather than leave his three-bedroom cottage on the farm, he rents out both the main house with tennis court and pool and the place in Maine. Granted, between the two, he gets almost $200,000 a year in rent, minus the upkeep. However, he gets more than that in a month for not doing anything.

When my uncle's granddaughter proudly told him that she and her husband had paid off their mortgage, he replied that they should never buy anything they could not pay for with cash. Obviously, he could have paid for it, but they knew he was too cheap to even be asked. He was so cheap that his wife, rather than tell him about a bill at the dress shop or jeweler, would borrow the money from my grandmother's housekeeper. She would then complain to my grandmother that things were so tough that they had to eat chipped beef every night. (They did have a cook and a maid.) My grandmother would then give her a nice check with which she would repay the housekeeper. The housekeeper was the family banker, it seems. Any time anyone wanted to spend more than their allowance on something, they would just call Sadie.

However, when economizing, don't go overboard, and don't talk about it. I knew a social climber who was very proud of his economizing. He would give presents from a warehouse store, not because he thought the present was good, just because it was on sale. He should have just given his presents directly to the charity shop because that is usually where they ended up. In his case, it wasn't the thought. It was the gift.

Another time, people left a house present for some friends who had let them use their summer place. It was a questionable item. The resort where the house was had a shop run by a local charity. They took it there. They were not the first donor of the item.

Now with more and more states levying heavy taxes aimed at the rich, many are moving to states that do not have income or inheritance tax. In the East, New Hampshire and Florida are two of the favorites. I knew of someone in Vermont who said for what they paid the state in income tax in one year, they could buy a place in Florida and set up residency. They haven't yet. However, when some states aim at the very rich, they are killing the golden goose.

Another way rich people save, particularly when shopping in high-sales-tax states like New York, is to have their purchases sent out of state. If they do not have an out-of-state residence, they will send it to out-of-state friends. It seems silly when you are spending thousands on clothing to begrudge a couple of hundred in sales taxes. However, that is how the rich stay rich.

Often they will spend lots of money where they could save and save where they should spend. They will spend thousands on a dress or club dues but then go to Walmart for paper products or drive for miles to get cheaper gas. Some will send their maids to the market, loaded down with coupons for things they do not need. These are called "idiosyncrasies" in rich people. Money is what makes the rich eccentric rather than just off-balance.

Basically, old money likes a bargain like anyone else. They hate being overcharged just because they are rich and, if they find out, will never repeat the experience. Once, a respected contractor was working in a town known for its rich inhabitants. One of his suppliers wanted to charge more for goods for people in that town. He refused and never used the supplier again. He knew what would happen if word got out, and he always asked, "Why should someone pay more for the same thing just because they are rich?" He always had work in that community. Overcharging does not happen as much as rich people suspect, but it does happen—and more often than it should.

15

The Little Darlings (Children and Pets)

Rich people seem to grow up together, thrown together by virtue of their parents' friends, where they go in the summer or winter, etc. Even as they grow up and stop attending each others' birthday or Halloween parties, or if they grew up going to Mount Desert but now go to Southampton, they keep the memories, and when they run into old friends at a coming-out party or at some resort, it is like old times. As a social climber, you will not have this familiarity, but just remember to be yourself and be gracious. If you have children, hopefully they will have this advantage, if you are successful.

It is important that children have some discipline and know that there are times, like the cocktail hour, that are adult times. However, don't be as strict about this as the fellow whose son came in during adult time. Before he could say anything, his father said, "Not now. It's adult time." What the boy was going to say was that their boat at the end of the dock was sinking.

With children, it is important to start them off early. Instill good manners and good taste in them as soon as they can understand. Think about how you want them educated. It will make all the difference in the world to them where they go to school. Public education can be fine, especially for the early years. However, if there is a good day school available, that might be the right choice for social climbers. You and your children will meet more people that way. And if there is a dancing class or sports team, they will be more likely to be invited if they are at private school, especially if you are not very socially prominent. For high school, they can either remain in their day school or perhaps go away to a good boarding school. There are a wide variety of boarding schools around the country, especially in the East. There they will be introduced to a wider variety of cultures and will be more immersed in education and cultural development. They may be invited to visit different parts of the world and will gain more social exposure. However, be sure that they are stable enough to go off on their own and not fall into bad habits.

As for higher education, it used to be thought that it was wasted on girls, who would marry and raise children. My grandmother thought that "university women" were overbearing and pretentious. My sisters were sent to two-year colleges and then to the Sorbonne, over their protests. They are both quite smart and would have done very well at four-year colleges. As it turned out, both did work outside of their homes for most of their lives because they enjoyed it. However, the lack of a college education was a hindrance. Times have evolved, fortunately. My nieces attended some of the best universities and went on to get graduate degrees.

Remember this saying: "Little pitchers have big ears." Children are apt to repeat whatever they hear, anytime and anyplace. If you and your spouse are having any sort of discussion about money, people, or whatever that you may not want everyone to hear, save it for when you are alone. Otherwise, the children are bound to blab it out, either to the servants or, worse, their friends.

Money is a topic that you must teach your children to avoid. They certainly should not let the amount of money a person has be the measure of that person. And remind them that no matter how much money they have, there is always someone with more money. The trick with children is to make them feel loved and secure, no matter what. If they are not comfortable with themselves, they will never be happy.

When they are old enough, it does not hurt to make them get a summer job, even for part of the summer. They can even work where you have your summer place. It builds character and makes them appreciate what work is. It can give them a better idea of what they want to do for a career.

Do not overindulge them. They should appreciate everything they have. When I was growing up, unless it was dinner party, I had to help clear the table. It was made clear to me that the staff was not there for just my benefit. When I was very small, I would even dust the legs of the tables and chairs for the housekeepers who suffered from arthritis. I was never told that we were rich, and it never occurred to me that we were. I just never thought about it.

Some friends of mine were at their summer camp in the Adirondacks. It was a lovely remote island but rustic—no dishwasher. Each night one of the children was to do the dishes. One night the family was still around the table when from the kitchen their son yelled, "Who stacked the dishes? Now I have to wash the top and the bottom!" Does we stack or is we class?

Make sure that your children understand that they are no better than anyone else just because you have money. Do not let them be label conscious. It is not good if they buy things because of the brand or label. They fall victim to fashion rather than style. If they are in a school where the students judge others by the labels they have, move them. This is a true sign of poor social climbing. It's not the place to find old money, and unless you wish them to spend their life as middle-class social climbers, it is not the place for them.

It is probably wise to get them started giving to charity at an early age. If they get an allowance or if they are given money as a gift, they should put some of it aside for a certain charity or church and put some of it into savings. Rich people are morally obligated to look after the less fortunate. This is something you should remember. It should not be a law—just a moral obligation.

A friend of mine had a deal with his children. Any money they saved during the year he would match at the end of the year. One of his sons wanted a new pair of ice-hockey skates. The boy's grandfather sent him a check for his November birthday to buy the skates. He thought about it and said, "Dad, if I save this until the end of the year, will you match it?" That was the deal, and the father stuck to it. The son not only got the matching funds; he was able to buy the skates on sale.

Many, but not all, old-moneyed people are very fond of pets, particularly dogs and horses. Some are even fonder of them than children. If you are also fond of dogs and horses, so much the better, but don't try to fake it. An animal is not a possession; it is a member of the family, especially dogs. It really doesn't matter if the dog is purebred or a rescue. People who rescue dogs are very commendable. What matters is that you are fond of it. Most who choose the purebred stick with the breed they start with. Often old money has bred the breed for generations.

Please do not dress your dog up like it is some kind of doll. Dogs have coats already. Unless you are living where the temperature is below zero, their natural coats will do. You can get an attractive collar and leash. Harry Barker is a good source. You should have a reputable vet wherever you have a house and take your pet's records with you.

The dog should be well-groomed and well-behaved. Other dog owners are very fussy about the dogs their pups are exposed to. Do not let your dog be rough or a bully. If your town has a nice dog park, feel free to take your dog there. Perhaps, as in Boca Grande, there is a time for small dogs and a time for big dogs. Do not make the mistake of taking your dog at the wrong time, especially if it is a big dog. If it is a very gentle dog, you can try to get away with it, but be careful.

In the area of horses, it is a bit more difficult. There are horses you keep, preferably on your farm, to ride cross-country, dressage, or show. Then there are hunters. It is not very difficult to get into a fox-hunt club. Most are looking for new members. But be sure that you are an accomplished rider and follow the strict rules of hunting. They are usually welcoming to those who can make the grade.

There are horse racing and polo, but racehorses and polo ponies are not considered pets. They are bred for the sport and are secondary to the sport.

As I said, if you do not truly love animals, do not get involved with them. They can grow on you, but they are not to be undertaken lightly.

16

The Power behind the Throne

It takes more than hard work to make a large fortune. It takes a lot of gumption and guts, a lot of luck, and risk taking. There are not many people born with all that it takes. Historically, men ruled the world of business and made the fortunes. However, it fell to their wives to rule the familial and social worlds. While more and more women have entered the business world in modern times, it is still the women who rule the family and society, for the most part.

It is up to the women to hold the family together in the face of adversity: be it an affair, a disaster, or a scandal. It is the women who have historically made personal sacrifices for the sake of the family. In recent times, the most famous of these is Hilary Clinton, denying to the last her husband's infidelity. No one knows what goes on behind the marital closed doors, but it is safe to say that these humiliations do not go unrewarded. True or not, Jacqueline Kennedy was allegedly paid $1 million to remain in her marriage in spite of her husband's dalliances. Her mother-in-law, Rose, remained silent and devout in spite of Mr. Kennedy's famed affairs with Hollywood beauties. Rose raised her children and ran her houses in Boston, Cape Cod, and Palm Beach with not so much as a whimper about the injustices done to her. Like with so many men who have the ego it takes to make a fortune, Mr. Kennedy's affairs had not as much to do with love as with pure lust and raw power. In the end, he came around and became faithful to his wife, whom he loved, and she nursed him through his feeble old age.

These women are remarkable for their calm demeanor and stoic inner strength. In the world of old money, of course, a wife has unrestricted use of the funds, which can ease the pain. If a husband spends all his time at work or elsewhere, a wife can ease her loneliness with charity work and charge cards. Usually the husband will accompany her to family functions and charity events in spite of everyone knowing about "another woman." Their private life is just that, no matter how many people know. It is something that "nice" people don't openly acknowledge.

Historically, the ultimate reward for women has been to see their children grow up to be successful in life and to love them unconditionally. Not all self-made men are wanderers, but for those who are, it is just another game.

There was one widow who ran the family newspaper after her husband's death. Her sons all worked at the paper, which made it easier for her to control them. When one son joined the army during World War II, she was so displeased that she cut his pay in half. It might not seem that drastic, but he had a wife and three young children to rear. Now that would be against the law. One of the political parties wanted to run another son for the United States Senate. At the time, senators were not well-paid and needed outside income. Such was her love for her sons and her wish that they remain nearby that she said not only would the family not support him, they would finance his opposition.

If you ever have any doubt as to who is in control of the social reins of a town, it is the women. Among them there may be a hierarchy, based on age, how long the family has been in society, what each woman's social and charitable achievements are, and, of course, popularity. Often the husband's wealth and importance are factors, but these are usually taken for granted. It is not wise to jump to conclusions about someone's status too soon. Wait until you have observed how they are greeted and treated by others and how others value their thoughts and opinions. These will be made very clear very quickly. Do not hitch your wagon to the wrong horse, or you will not get very far.

As I stated at the outset of this chapter, it takes more than hard work to make a large fortune. There are not many people born with all that it takes. Often, the children or grandchildren of the founder of the fortune have had a totally different life from that of the patriarch. Then he might openly show his disappointment or even disgust at what he perceives to be their lack of ambition or nerve. Unless tempered by a spousal counterpart, that can be very hard on the descendant, and a bout with alcohol or drugs may ensue, further shattering the family. However, the mother will almost always stand firmly by her child.

There are some exceptions, like Uncle Tim. These usually involve the marriage of a child not being acceptable to the parents, particularly the mother. The one sin a son can make in his mother's eyes is choosing a bride from a different social class, whom she sees as totally unsuitable for him. If the son goes through with the marriage, the mother may make the best of it. Or she may undermine the marriage every chance she gets. At any rate, it will take a lot of hard work and forgiveness to win over a scorned mother. It is almost as if this kind of marriage is seen as a rejection of his upbringing. Or maybe there is something more oedipal to it. If a daughter runs off with a surfer or the tennis pro, on the other hand, it can usually be handled with money. But a son's lack of discretion is almost always fatal. If the young lady is accepted at all, she is never made a welcome part of the family. I refer again to *The Two Mrs. Grenvilles.* The elder Mrs. Grenville made the best of it, and yet it still ended badly for everyone.

Be sure that this is the life you want, and take care that you always have in mind the consequences of the moves you make and the relationships you form.

17

IN FUNDS WE TRUST

Trust funds can solve all kinds of problems or lead to them. Until sometime in the last century, if someone made a fortune, it was typical to leave that fortune in a generation-skipping trust fund to avoid the dreaded death tax. Now it is illegal. However, thankfully, my dear old grandfather put his corporation in a trust for his grandchildren, to be divided on the death of his last child. It carried his wife in high style and did all right by his children. I say "thankfully" because, on hearing that all of Uncle Tim's money was tied up in a trust for his children, Olivia went a bit off-kilter. The upshot was Tim obtaining a large life-insurance policy, and over the twenty-two years that they were married, he put everything in her name. She lost almost everything after he died, of course. She died twenty years after he did—penniless. He should have left it in trust so that she couldn't squander it. So trust funds can be a saving grace—at least for your descendants.

At the other end of the spectrum is the case of an entrepreneur who made a fortune. His wife divorced him, getting some money and their son, and she moved back to Texas. He remarried and had another family. He set up a trust for his oldest son but never got around to funding it. He decided to do so on his deathbed. His second wife had him declared mentally incompetent, thus denying him the chance to enrich his oldest son. The son got five hundred dollars and no more.

There can be some guilt that comes with inheriting a large amount of money. For the life of me I don't understand it, but some very wealthy beneficiaries have even felt compelled to write about the burden of their wealth and what good they have done with it. Plenty of people have inherited fortunes and done wonderful things with them quietly. At any rate, I don't think it evokes much sympathy to complain about your large inheritance.

There are two schools of thought about raising children with trust funds. One is to tell them and let them share the responsibility early on. The other is not to tell them anything about it. Some friends of mine who had pots of money raised their children without telling them. There was no doubt about the fact that they were wealthy. When a child graduated from college, they would then present him or her with a BMW and the trust fund. They had eight children, and all are responsible and respected adults.

There are those who say that trust funds ruin people because they remove any ambition. I don't think that is true. Plenty of rich people work and don't just live off their inheritance. It's just nice to have the choice. But you have to be careful how you set it up, and if the trust is irrevocable, you should think everything through. There was an heir to a huge chemical fortune. His first wife gave him three lovely daughters. They all got trust funds, of course. But then his next wife gave him a son. He put all his material goods in a trust for the chosen one. However, he ended up divorcing that wife. That's when it got bad. His son was no longer the apple of his eye. But the trust was irrevocable. He spent a great deal of money trying in vain to break it. He finally sank his seventy-five-foot boat and let his houses in New York and Paris go unattended. His joy had turned to bitterness. He was finally able to break part of it.

To set up the fund, you will need to contact your lawyer. Rich people are always talking to their lawyer or their investment advisor. You can mention these conversations casually, but never overdo it. And make sure you have the right lawyer and investment advisor. It won't do to drop that you were talking to your lawyer, and his firm is on television advertising for clients seeking social security disability or settlement for mesothelioma.

And you have to be careful whom you leave as the trustees. In the case of a Palm Beach heir who married a showgirl and had a son, he left the wife and a prominent New York bank as trustees. The wife remarried a New York cop after the demise of the heir, and they lived the high life in Palm Beach. Unfortunately, allegedly with the bank's blessing, she raided the millions left in trust for her son. It was the Palm Beach scandal of the year.

Often banks have trust departments and will act as a cotrustee—for a fee. Depending on the size of the trust, you may want several trustees. My grandfather appointed his wife and all six children. In such a large group, they did not get along, but they were a good balance for each other. Unfortunately, as happens in many families, they wound up in court a few times. In the end it only depleted the trust to the benefit of the lawyers. And since they didn't trust each other, everyone had their own lawyer. Eventually, due to the deaths of the trustees, my generation started to take seats on the board. It did not get any better, and finally the court broke it into smaller trusts for each family. It was the first time that almost everyone was friendly in decades.

18

IMPORTANT THINGS TO KNOW

*A*s I said, any kind of information, useless and useful, is valuable. Oddly enough, much useful information—like how to change a tire or even how to do most household repairs—eludes rich people, leaving them at the mercy of servicepeople. One lady I knew growing up was separated from her husband and on her own for the first time in her life. Someone told her that the light bulb was burned out in one of her lamps. Her first thought was to call Public Service Electric & Gas. Another family couldn't get their pool house cool enough in the summer. The electrician pointed out that the air-conditioning works better if you have the sliding doors shut. These are not stupid people; they just live on a different level.

However, there are many things that old money just grows up with and, therefore, like good manners, are second nature to them. If they hear "Claridges," they know that it is a luxury hotel in London. If someone mentions "the Brook" or "the Links," they know that these are men's clubs in Manhattan. They know where the Eastern Shore is as well as where the Cape is. They know shopping on Worth Avenue as opposed to Newbury Street. They know where the Isabella Gardiner Museum is and where the Corcoran Gallery is and where the Amon Carter Museum is. They know the Everglades (a club in Palm Beach) and the Maidstone (a club in East Hampton). These seem to be useless facts, but in conversation, they can be invaluable.

Much of these facts you can learn. It may be hard work, but you should enjoy it if you are a good and authentic social climber. You should break your studies down into categories so that you don't get the subjects confused.

For shopping, you can start with the obvious high-end stores, but there are lesser-known places as well. You will get to know them either by word of mouth or reading about them. Read your *Departures* magazine; get *Town & Country*, *Vanity Fair* (great for gossip, not for politics), and *Saveur*. Get some local magazines, like *Palm Beach or Avenue*.

You should also read some biographies of authentic old money as well as noted social climbers. The novels of Dominick Dunne are based on real events, so try those. If you don't have time to read whole books, again, you can Google names. Be careful to double-check the facts.

You should know how to dance gracefully—both men and women. Old money goes to dancing school starting in grade school. I remember that every boy said he hated going to the Barclay classes, but they proved very useful in life. In the eighth or ninth grade, they start going to cotillions, and then in high school, there are holiday dances. Eventually there are coming-out balls, dinner dances, and weddings. Find a reputable ballroom-dance school. Learn the basic dances (waltz, lindy, fox-trot, Charleston, twist— the teachers will know what you need to learn) and learn how to move rhythmically and gracefully. Not even all old money is good at it, but if you are good, it will make you a welcome addition at dances and balls.

You should also be familiar with the arts, even in a basic way. You may not enjoy all of them, but on the other hand, you may like some more than you thought, as you are more exposed. The arts I am talking about are opera, symphony, ballet, and the visual arts, which include paintings, prints, photographs, fabrics, ceramics, glass, and sculpture. You can listen to the opera and symphony on recordings, but you should experience at least a few of each. The ballet you can see on film, but again, you should experience a few. For the visual arts, you should buy a Janson *History of Art* and look through it. Subscribe to major auction-house catalogs. Read the development of each period. Visit museums and historical sights. If you feel a fondness for any of these things, delve deeper. You don't have to have season tickets or own a Monet to enjoy the arts. If there is a local college or university, you might think about auditing courses.

There was a time, before the Second World War, when it was de rigueur to be a patron of one or more artists. There were artists like John Singer Sargent, who was famous for painting portraits of society folk. Some friends of my grandparents even had an artist's studio at their house on Cape Cod, where they had Robert Henri, among others, paint. They would have artists do their Christmas cards and other such niceties. While I was away at college, a couple moved to my hometown. They bought a lovely old house with a ballroom. At one of their cocktail parties in the ballroom, they unveiled a portrait of themselves—in bed, in a postcoital state. It made an impression—a bad one. They eventually moved on but later reportedly got a divorce. Who got custody of the portrait? And is that really an heirloom you would want to leave for your children and grandchildren? I hardly think it is destined to hang in a museum beside a John Singer Sargent portrait.

Sophistication is just knowledge. Learn everything you can, and you can be as sophisticated as anyone. The more you know, the fewer mistakes you will make.

Think about what you are getting into. It may look wonderful to be a part of the upper reaches of society. It is not always the case. Often, money causes stress and unhappiness rather than happiness and a life of ease. Having a last name that is synonymous with wealth or with an international corporation can bear a big responsibility. Everything you do is a reflection on the family name. There are those who use it to full advantage, but there are also many who run from the name. And it can be hard on those who do not measure up to the family standards.

As Eric Hoffer said, "In times of change learners inherit the earth; while the learned find themselves beautifully equipped to deal with a world that no longer exists."

Although change is inevitable, old money often would rather resist it. When you are privileged and used to life being a certain way, it can be difficult to see the institutions you have grown up with change. However, nothing ever remains totally the same. The world is constantly changing—faster now than ever—and people have to change with it. However, these rules still apply. While old money can afford to resist, to keep things just as they "always have been," most accept the changes and learn to cope. Certainly many older people do not want to change and live out their lives resisting. The servants and the clubs and the universities, the debutante balls, and large properties have defined their lives.

However, those who move with the times are much happier. Younger people who refuse the changes and stick to the old snobbism seem to be stilted and out of touch. If you run into these people, don't waste your time. Their way of life is over, and they are deathly afraid of social climbers, as they see you as a further threat to their existence. Unfortunately for them, their peers see them as the anachronisms they are. They will always be accepted unless they perform some unimaginable gaffe. But they will never be respected. They can be amusing. But they can also be bitter and nasty.

Always remember to make people comfortable. If someone is comfortable with you, you have a good chance of becoming friends. Don't overshadow them or sell yourself too hard. I will close as I opened, with the words of my grandfather: "Keep a sense of humor and be kind to everybody. Don't develop superior traits, even if you feel you are superior. The smartest folks I have known have been the simplest, those who understood that we're living in a dumb world but made the best of it. Be affable to damfools who think they are important; you never can tell where and when they can do you a good turn. Nobody is really of much importance because the whole life of the greatest man is brief. Always keep in mind that life is too short for you to be small."

As you go forth to try to get into the world of the rich and mighty, remember to be yourself, if your new self. Have plenty of self-confidence.

If you don't enjoy it or if you begin to suffer from anxiety and depression, find another way of life. In more of my grandfather's words, "Life is the great thing, after all."

Appendices

Accoutrements for

Social Climbers

*Denotes optional

For Ladies

A good gold bracelet
Good pearls
A Nantucket basket* (You have to go to Nantucket to get it)
Hermes Kelly bag*
Burberry raincoat
Belgian shoes
Lillys
Stubbs & Wooten shoes*
A simple black dress
Hermes scarves
Ferragamo shoes
Jean Schlumberger enamel jewelry*
Cashmere sweaters
Bracelets from the Rock Shop in Bar Harbor, Maine*
Monogrammed L. L. Bean sailing bag

For Gentlemen

Blue blazer
Khakis
Gray flannels
A good Swiss watch
Hermes ties
Vineyard Vines ties*
Nantucket reds—preferably from Murray's Toggery in Nantucket
Polo shirts
Gucci shoes in brown and/or black (black can be worn with a tuxedo)
Cordovan penny loafers
Sperry boat shoes
Belgian shoes in brown with black trim*
Boxers, not briefs
Socks that don't reveal leg when seated
A proper tuxedo
Burberry raincoat
Barbour jacket
Polo coat*
Chesterfield
Studs and cuff links
Cashmere sweaters
Monogrammed linen handkerchiefs (always have one available in your jacket pocket)
White flannels*
Monogrammed L. L. Bean sailing bag
Monogrammed sterling silver jigger (often given out as groomsmen's presents)
A pair of silver hairbrushes*

Things Social Climbers Should Avoid

For Ladies

Absolutely no tattoos
No piercings, except the ears
Foot jewelry—leave it for the Gypsies
Questionable swimwear—brief bikinis and thongs
Tennis bracelets
Metallic footwear during the day
Anything Vuitton unless it is obviously old—no longer the domain of the very rich, as good knockoffs are available on the street corner
Plastic jewelry
Plastic shoes
Cheap perfume
Big hair
Too much makeup
Breast enhancements
Botox—it never looks natural

For Gentlemen

Absolutely no tattoos or piercings

Speedos (unless you are in the Olympics) or other re-
vealing swim attire
Armless shirts of all kinds
Gold chains and most other jewelry
Facial hair
Bad teeth
Socks that do not meet the pant leg
Clip-on ties
Polyester of any sort
Socks in warm weather
Toupees and hair dye
Botox
Sideburns
Ponytails

Old-Money Staples

Deviled eggs
BLTs
Vichyssoise
Filet mignon
Asparagus
Artichokes
Hollandaise sauce
Béarnaise sauce
Lamb chops
Venison
Quail
Smoked pheasant
Chicken salad
Brownies
Devon cream
Petit fours
Crème brûlée
Vanilla ice cream with fresh strawberries
Baked Alaska
Floating island
Smoked salmon
Pâté

Hot dogs
A great hamburger
Chicken hash
Omelets
Eggs Benedict
Any soufflé
Aspic
Consommé
Turtle soup with sherry
Bouillon
Black bean soup
Chocolate mousse
Dover sole
Oyster stew
Mulligatawny
Stilton cheese and port
Tournedos rossini
Lobster
Foie gras (and Chateau d'Yquem)
Truffles
Cornichons
Beurre blanc
Capers
Absolutely fresh fruit and vegetables